MW01235787

The Book Business Book:

Building an Author Persona for Fiction Authors

Broken Glass Publishing, Evansville, IN

The Book Business Book

Building an Author Persona for Fiction Authors

Lindblom & Shofner

Dedicated to …

… the dreams.

Acknowledgments:

As I sit here staring at my two computer screens, my music loud and distracting, and my dogs poking me to remind me it is time for fetch, I reflect on those that waltzed through my life and profoundly changed me. Thanks to Paul, Sharon, and Jon for teaching me perseverance; Laura and Jennifer for teaching me unquestioning faith and patience; Janet for always dreaming bigger and better and dragging me with her; and finally to Virgie and Valley for giving me back my hope. My thanks to all of them for showing me that success is in the eye of the beholder.

This is not an easy business. It takes a bit of your soul day by day. This business will teach you, slam you, drown you, lift you up and remind you every day to "Be careful what you ask for." I am thankful for every day that the business enfolded me, cared for me, promoted me, and taught me that anyone can accomplish anything they want, if they really want it.

My greatest thanks and appreciation go to my family because I couldn't have survived over fifteen years in this business without a single one of them. My oldest for his no nonsense, down to earth approach to life that keeps me securely on the ground. My youngest for his pushing, pushing and more pushing, making me see things differently. My wonderful husband and partner, who picks me up and brushes me off, kissing away every hurt and pain, and for those rose colored glasses that he sees me through, that keep me securely on the pedestal he places me on.

Heidi Christine

Thanks to my book editor, H. Christine Lindblom, who helped me move to the next step in my writing career, all the while screaming, "SIU," in the nicest way possible; to my publisher, Terry Mominee, who laughs at my jokes, listens to my whining and still speaks to me, and to all the people I worked with during my thirty years, plus in the corporate world who imparted the valuable knowledge included in this book.

Virgie

INTRODUCTION

You did it! You have a book! The cover is perfect, the interior looks great; you have it listed with the distributor and online stores. All your copyright paperwork is registered with the Library of Congress. WOW! That is an accomplishment, a unique and powerful one at that! Everyone is going to buy it because you did it, right? I only wish it was that easy. You need to promote, promote, promote!

Not to undermine your accomplishments, because your accomplishment is a great feat, but if you are on the shelf next to a best selling author, it becomes a competition of names. Whose book is the reader going to buy? Theirs or yours? You may both offer the same value, the same quality, and the same type of story, so why would a consumer choose theirs over yours? Because the best-selling authors have a track record, have a great deal of promotion, name recognition, and are therefore, the safer purchase. Your book may be better written, but if they don't know you, they aren't taking a chance.

The rewards can be epic!

So how do you fix this? Well, you do what the Big Boys in the publishing industry do. You become a promoting, published author and not just another name in the jungle. You do the same thing that put authors on the *New York Times Best Sellers* list, *Publishers Weekly,* and the *Midwest Book Review*. You spend time on the promotions that sell 10,000 units before the book even hits the street. You make the deals for subsidiary and foreign rights and book clubs, big and small screen producers, paperback rights, ebooks etc.

Is this a guarantee for success? No. There are no guarantees. As our parents used to say, "Hard work, diligence, and innovation are what breeds success." If you work hard you can have it all. *The Book Business Book* will provide you a map of how to apply the qualities of our parents' motto to your success as a writer.

There is only one rule for using this book: "Do what you can." If your book is already available to the public, it DOES NOT deny you any avenue. There are lots of options, but the basic framework outlined in this book will work. The title of this book is *The Book Business Book* and the word **Business** is really very important. This is a highly competitive and expensive business. Many entrepreneurial authors enter this business without a plan for goals, accomplishments and eventual retirement. Most of the information in this book is not new and it is not earth shattering. What this book does it take the guess work out of how to get started and gives you steps to move forward.

The thing to remember about this business is that instant gratification does not exist. You didn't write your book overnight. You typed late hours on the computer or writing tablet because your story needed to be told. You celebrated when you finished and breathed a sigh of relief as you thought of all the hours you put into your project. Unfortunately, no one told you that the writing of the book may have been the least time consuming portion of your journey to becoming a successful author. Selling your book will take twice as long as writing it (on average). Selling your book is a business:

As defined by *Princeton*, "Business" means: **An organization operated with the objective of making a profit from the sale of goods or services.**

The buyers are there to make a profit, you are there to make a profit - and that takes time. Lots of time.

The face of book publishing has changed dramatically in the past few years. Instead of having a lot of companies that might take a chance on an unpublished or unknown writer, the publishers have consolidated and only the few are invited into their inner circle. Even if the companies are willing to take a chance on someone who doesn't have a track record or isn't a celebrity, the author will be asked to not only participate, but also have a number of marketing tools in place to support any type of publicity or promotions they might provide.

In addition, the internet is changing the face of publishing and will continue to move the industry forward, and is growing at an amazing rate. The current generation has access to computers not only at school, but students are allowed to take them home to complete assignments. Ebooks are no longer a possibility but a reality that authors can take advantage of. Although this is another avenue available for publishing, more will be expected of authors, including pages on social networks, blogs, author web sites, and whatever else can be used for marketing and support.

The run of a nonfiction book title is about three years. After that you have saturated your market and need to release a 2nd edition. The run of a hard cover fiction book title is about eighteen months. After that you release the title as a paperback. As a paperback, the run can be much longer, but the older it gets the harder it is to market. Market viability for a title is becoming shorter and shorter as technology advances. Hard cover books are rapidly becoming a thing of the past. Between the first writing of this chapter and today, hard covers have disappeared at epic rates.

By the end of *The Book Business Book* you will have some tools to help you put your marketing and publicity package together. If you haven't done so already, you will also need to decide if you only have one book inside or if you want a career as an author.

Marketing a book is akin to getting another full time job or changing careers. To begin with you are going to be asked some hard questions. Questions about things that you may take for granted or just do without thought. This questionnaire will be repeated at the end of this book and it is something to hold close to you, so that you can answer it frequently as things in your life change. If you have a partner by any definition, sit down with them and go over it. Get their input. What you do is going to affect them also, and it is imperative that you personally understand the enormity of what you are undertaking, and that it will have a profound influence on the rest of your life, no matter the outcome.

So, the journey will be long, the trials great, and sometimes you may feel that you are living your own epic adventure, complete with battles and battle fatigue. However, the rewards can also be epic! You have written from your heart, from your passion, a book. You are brave enough to send it out into the world. Ride this experience to its fullest, have the most fun possible and enjoy your time in the sun.

What is going on in your life right now? (List your top 5 priorities)

_____

_____

_____

_____

_____

Do you have a partner? (Spouse, girlfriend, boyfriend, fiance.)

       Yes   No

Do you have children?

       Yes   No

List 5 ways that marketing will affect them. (Think in both the positive and the negative. For example, we will spend our summer vacations at book signings, but book signings only take a couple of hours, so look at all the neat stuff they are going to see along the way.)

_____

_____

_____

_____

_____

Are you going to keep your current job?

       Yes   No

Can you pay your bills and pay for your marketing if you work part time?

       Yes   No

Can you quit your job and become a full time author and marketing extraordinaire?

        Yes   No

Describe what your marketing career looks like.

_____

_____

_____

_____

_____

_____

List 5 things you expect to get our of your efforts.

_____

_____

_____

_____

_____

_____

Was this just a fun project that you have completed and now you can move on?

        Yes   No

Chapter One: Creating A Plan

There are several things to consider when looking at your market. The first is that 75% of all books are purchased by females, according to Jane Friedman formerly of *Writer's Digest*. This means that not only are women your target readers, but they also purchase the books for the men in their lives. Taking that basic information, let us start to define your buying market.

You may think that the statistic above doesn't affect your book, but think again. Consider the case of a young adult science fiction novel. The primary reading audience is going to be preteen and teenage boys. If vampires and a little bit of romance are added to the mix, then girls of the same age join the reading audience. The problem with marketing to preteens is that they don't actually have the money, their parents do. So marketing has to attract the reading preteens but also be attractive to their parents (generally their mothers) who flash the credit card to buy the book.

Remember that you are a writer with an unlimited imagination.

Another example: A children's pictorial, with a reading marketing whose age group can't even read. The buying audience is most likely the grandmothers. So the marketing goal is to get that child to pick it up off the shelf and ask the grandparent to buy it. The grandparent quickly reviews the book, scanning for a moral value presented in such a way that the child doesn't know it is learning. Therefore, the layout of the book is just as important as the words you are using to write the story. A majority of children's books are purchased by a child begging to have it. Grandparents buy more than parents, and after the initial "My child has to read for school," children's book sales decline.

Think about the reading level of your market. Do not assume the book they purchase is all the reader reads. Individuals use different types of reading choices for different aspects of their lives. "Brain Candy" is a series of bestselling books written for reading levels between a 5th grade level and 7th grade level. The content is what makes it adult. It is easy to read and you can put it down, pick it up months later and not have missed a thing. "Literary" is either fiction or nonfiction that causes you to think, create, or supports a social conscience and pulls at the moral fiber of who you are. These are written at a higher level, either the senior year of high school or your freshman year of college.

To create a general plan there are some simple questions that need to be answered and worked through. The answers to these questions will help form in your mind what is important to you about your book, therefore what will be important to your buyers. Remember if you are excited, positive and upbeat, your energy will cause everyone around you to be excited, positive and upbeat, resulting in them parting with their hard earned cash for your book. It doesn't matter what format the book is in print, ebook, or audio, your excitement will travel through you to the reader.

There are a lot of questions that break down your overall story into detailed micro bits that will be used for all your marketing copy. When you are answering the questions, keep it honest, but remember that you are a writer with an unlimited imagination, so use your words to create a unique, entertaining and interesting bit to attract your toughest buyer.

Goals for Your Writing Career

Is this book your "One Hit Wonder?" Is this the one story you have to tell? The only one you will sell? If you answered "Yes" to this, then you are done with this section. (Go to page 8)

Which other stories do you have to tell? Are they sequels to the one you've written? (TIP: Some of the biggest authors weren't well known until their 7th, 8th or 12th title. Their earlier books sell well only because of press they received on a later book.)

6
_____

_____

_____

_____

_____

_____

Do you have other genres you want to explore writing? This is your wish list, someone is paying you to write so what would you write? (TIP: Take your time and don't limit yourself to one particular genre, or publication style. Just because you enjoy writing novels doesn't mean you aren't going to enjoy writing short stories, screenplays, stage plays, descriptions, copy or even editorials.)

_____

_____

_____

_____

_____

_____

_____

_____

_____

Where do you see yourself in 5 years? In 10 years? What have you accomplished? Where do you see your main income stemming from? (TIP: Include income from workshops, speaking engagements, coaching, book sales, movie rights, more books, nonfiction, and subsidiary rights. These may just be wish lists, but this is where you make your wishes!)

_____

_____

_____

_____

_____

_____

_____

_____

_____

_____

_____

Where do you want to be 20 years from now? Will you be writing in a quiet corner of a restaurant where no one bothers you, but they point at you as a world famous, world class author? Do you want your own TV talk show, your own publishing company, or just to sail away into the sunset? (TIP: You are only limited by your imagination so dream big and then you can be realistic about the work involved.)

_____

_____

_____

_____

_____

_____

_____

_____

_____

What is going to make it so I want to read this book?

Your toughest selling audience is a guy. Now try a middle aged guy who isn't interested in anything more than football, beer and mud bogging. Even if you are writing a general fiction that blows something up every other page and shoots someone in between, they won't buy your book. So when thinking of how to sell the book and the ideas that you have, focus on your hardest sell.

Don't focus on the well written or the well ordered. Do not focus on your style or your reasons for writing the story. No one really cares about that. All they care about is the story. What about your story is going to make someone want to read the book? Don't weigh everything down with detail and plot twists. You have ten words to sell your book so please tell me why I want to read your book.

Give me your plot in 25 words.

_____

_____

_____

Give me your protagonist in 25 words.

_____

_____

_____

Give me your antagonist in 25 words.

_____

_____

_____

Now make them all one paragraph.

_____

_____

_____

_____

_____

Now cut out all the extra words you don't need.

_____

_____

_____

_____

Simplify to 10 words or less and please tell me why I want to read your book.

_____

_____

_____

What is important about this book?

Each author writes with a purpose of importance within the story. If your main character has had a tragedy such as her husband passing away, or the loss of a child. Then the lesson of the book may be something as simple as moving on. The lesson and importance of the book /story is simple. Don't think it will be anything more than the simple things in life that are repeated again and again on our television screens, on our movie screens, or in the books we read or the lessons we teach our children, instill in our friends or inspire in our colleagues. These are the stories that sell. These are the things that people relate to, how they connect to you and then to your stories. Keep it simple, keep it passionate, and keep it twenty-five words or less.

Write as much as you want about why this story is important. Make sure to include all the reasons it is important and mark the milestones of the journey that create the desire for another to travel the same path.

_____

_____

_____

_____

_____

_____

_____

Remove any extra words.

_____

_____

_____

_____

_____

_____

_____

_____

_____

Now create complex sentences from your simple sentences.

_____

_____

_____

10 _____

_____

Reduce until you have 25 words or less.

_____

_____

_____

Read it aloud to check for continuity, flow and complete thoughts.

Rewrite.

_____

_____

_____

What makes your story unique?

As we stated above, the stories are generally the same basic theme that makes people relate and show success and perseverance with each life changing event. What makes your story unique is your presentation. Do we learn how to overcome death in the underworld of the fourth moon of Zander or do we fight off the evil infiltrator to save our true love in the wilds of the Wyoming frontier, as he tries to tie her to the railroad tracks, yet again? Although the overly simplified task may be the same as every other book on the shelves right now, how is yours different from everyone else's?

What makes your protagonist someone that the reader will root for?

_____

_____

_____

_____

_____

_____

11

What makes your antagonist someone the reader will hate?

_____

_____

_____

_____

_____

What makes your setting different? A lot of stories happen in apartments or cities. What makes the setting characteristic of the group of characters playing out your story?

_____

_____

_____

_____

_____

How have you woven the old thread of story through a new setting?

_____

_____

_____

_____

_____

There was a time when magic or sorcery, werewolves and vampires were all great tools to add spice and change the way information and hurdles were delivered to the protagonist. These are now blase and moving out of the accepted corridors of the readers who are tired of it. Noting you will still have fanatics if you use it. So how are you introducing the same old fad with a new twist that will be not only believable, but offer a twist to the readers who are bored.

Write a description of how yours is different.

_____

_____

_____

_____

_____

_____

_____

_____

Remove any extra words.

_____

_____

_____

_____

Now create complex sentences from your simple sentences.

_____

_____

_____

_____

_____

_____

Reduce again to meet word count.

_____

_____

_____

Read it aloud to check for continuity, flow and complete thoughts.

Rewrite.

_____

_____

_____

What makes this story believable?

As an author, your imagination knows no bounds. As readers, neither do ours. With the increase in television shows that relate scientific information to the everyday world of what we do, we as a general audience have a better basic knowledge of the world of science as it relates to us. So when you are creating your story, does the order and progression make sense? Could a reader take a diagram and follow the thread of your story from its inception to its completion? Your imagination can run wild, and in no way do we want to put a hamper on it, but it has to be believable.

Where does your story start?

_____

_____

_____

_____

_____

_____

Where does your story end?

_____

_____

_____

_____

_____

_____

List the 5 major plot twists followed by the 3 steps that make each plot twist possible.

_____

_____

_____

_____

_____

14

_____

_____

_____

_____

_____

Collect all of your sentences and write them in one paragraph.

_____

_____

_____

_____

_____

_____

_____

_____

_____

Remove any extra words.

_____

_____

_____

_____

_____

_____

_____

_____

_____

_____

Now create complex sentences from your simple sentences.

_____

_____

_____

_____

_____

Reduce again to meet word count. (10 words)

_____

_____

_____

Read it aloud to check for continuity, flow and complete thoughts.

Rewrite

_____

_____

_____

Who is talking?

Most readers get confused when the author goes back and forth between speakers. As writers we remember that if it starts past tense, it should stay past tense. If it is first person it should stay first person. Sometimes though, a scene seems better from the antagonist's point of view or a secondary character's point of view, thereby changing the person who is telling the story and confusing the readers. The speaker should be either the most powerful person in the book, or an onlooker that isn't directly involved.

Who is your speaker?

_____

_____

Why does your speaker have to be this character?

_____

16 _____

_____

_____

_____

_____

_____

_____

_____

What does your speaker bring to the story that another character couldn't?

_____

_____

_____

_____

_____

_____

_____

Why should your reader like this speaker?

_____

_____

_____

_____

_____

_____

_____

_____

_____

_____

How can your reader relate to this speaker?

_____

_____

_____

_____

_____

_____

_____

_____

_____

Collect all of your sentences and write them in one paragraph.

_____

_____

_____

_____

_____

_____

_____

_____

_____

_____

Remove any extra words.

18 _____

_____

_____

_____

_____

Now create complex sentences from your simple sentences.

_____

_____

_____

_____

_____

Reduce again to meet word count. (25 words)

_____

_____

_____

Read it aloud to check for continuity, flow and complete thoughts.

Rewrite

_____

_____

_____

Where is this stuff happening?

Where stuff is happening is important to your reading base. If you are writing a romance that includes a Boston Red Sox player you would not market it at a New York Yankees game and expect to sell it. If you have written an off world romance it would be very difficult to market it to the Red Hat Society of Climax, Kansas (yes it is a real city), whose total population by the 2010 census was 72 people, up from 64 at the 2000 census.

So where does your story happen?

_____

_____

_____

_____

_____

_____

_____

_____

_____

What is the main industry of the people in your story?

_____

_____

_____

_____

_____

_____

What is the main social activity of people in your story?

_____

_____

_____

_____

What is the main interest of people in your story?

_____

_____

_____

_____

How does all of this lend credence to your story?

_____

_____

_____

_____

_____

_____

What region would be best for you to sell your book and why?

_____

_____

_____

_____

_____

_____

Collect all of your sentences and write them in one paragraph.

Remove any extra words.

Now create complex sentences from your simple sentences.

Reduce again to meet word count. (10 words)

Read it aloud to check for continuity, flow and complete thoughts.

Rewrite

Is your story line interesting?

Your story line has to be interesting from the beginning to end. You have less than 7 words to catch the reader and less than a page to make them want to get to the next one. So make sure that your general story line is attractive to your buying audience.

So why is your story line interesting?

_____

_____

_____

_____

_____

_____

_____

_____

22 _____

_____

_____

List 3 new styles, jumps, twists or tricks that create a flowing, non stop story line. Support each of these 3 with at least 2 items that support what you are doing.

_____

_____

_____

_____

_____

_____

_____

_____

_____

_____

List 5 action points in your story line that will keep the reader turning pages. List 3 action points to support each of your cited action points.

_____

_____

_____

_____

_____

_____

_____

_____

_____

_____

_____

_____

Collect all of your sentences and write them in one paragraph.

_____

_____

_____

_____

_____

_____

_____

_____

_____

_____

_____

_____

_____

_____

_____

_____

Remove any extra words.

_____

_____

_____

_____

_____

_____

Now create complex sentences from your simple sentences.

_____

_____

_____

_____

24

_____

Reduce again to meet word count. (7 words)

_____

_____

Read it aloud to check for continuity, flow and complete thoughts.

Rewrite.

_____

_____

Is your back story believable?

Your back story is as important as your main story line. It helps to support your main story line, creates some diversity and adds depth to your overall story. When you are writing about your back story, make sure to cover the points that make it a plot line that stands alone yet supports your main story line.

So why is your back story interesting?

_____

_____

_____

_____

_____

List 3 new styles, jumps, twists or tricks that support your main story line. Support each of these 3 with at least 2 items that support the progression of your back story.

_____

_____

_____

_____

_____

_____

_____

_____

_____

_____

_____

_____

_____

_____

_____

_____

List 3 action points in your back story that will keep the reader turning pages. List at least one action point to support each of your cited action points.

———————————————————
———————————————————
———————————————————
———————————————————
———————————————————
———————————————————
———————————————————
———————————————————
———————————————————
———————————————————
———————————————————

Collect all of your sentences and write them in one paragraph.

———————————————————
———————————————————
———————————————————
———————————————————
———————————————————
———————————————————
———————————————————
———————————————————
———————————————————
———————————————————

Remove any extra words.

———————————————————
———————————————————
———————————————————
———————————————————

Now create complex sentences from your simple sentences.

_____

_____

_____

_____

_____

Reduce again to meet word count. (7 words)

_____

_____

Read it aloud to check for continuity, flow and complete thoughts.

Rewrite

Chapter Two: Analyzing Your Market Competition

Do you know who your competition is? Your greatest competitors are the books directly around yours on the shelf. If you write contemporary romance and the last name you use starts with an R, your book will be placed near Nora Roberts, which makes her your competition. If you write mystery and the last name you use starts with B, your book will be placed near Dan Brown, which makes him your competition.

Go to your local bookstore and sit near your section. The information you are collecting is the base of your marketing plan. It will help you define your direct market and expand your market to include those individuals who may not be interested in your genre but like your story subject. Observe how people buy the books. Do they look at the front cover and then switch to the back? Do they open the book randomly and read? What do they carry to the counter?

Your target audiences are the people who are going to buy your book. You need to know their characteristics which are the foundation of where you spend your marketing dollar. If you have written a children's book, look at who buys them, not who reads them. If you have written a cook book, look at who buys them, not who uses them, most of those are gifts. Spend time in your bookstore and watch. Watch what people look at, how they look at books. Watch what they buy and how they decide what is worth their money. A couple of hours, two or three times a year in a bookstore watching, is the best way to keep you in touch with your buyers.

Decide what you need to do to compete.

Now who is your direct competition? Are you going to have to read them? I believe this is a must! Knowing your competition is essential, what their style is, how they work the plot, what the interior of their book looks like, and their cover can go a long way to helping you decide what you need to do to compete with authors who have already been published. Big publishing houses spend tons of marketing research money to find out what a reader will buy: What colors sell, what the interiors should resemble and how to part the client from their dollar. Remember that 75% of all books are bought by women. Even if they are buying them for men, the women are buying them. So when you look at this question you need to think about income levels, types of hobbies, likes, dislikes, location of book stores, and placement of books on the shelves.

Recognize Your Competition

Who are you sitting next to on the shelf? If you are writing contemporary romance or general fiction and your last name is Ro-something, chances are you are sitting next to Nora Roberts. Guess what? She is your competition. Don't let this intimidate you, let it flatter you. You are good enough to be next to one of the top selling authors of all time. Your book is right there next to the best of the best, in sales and in marketing. Use it to your advantage. It is truly a positive move.

Remember these people are your future readers.

Now go to the local bookstore, pull up a chair in an empty corner, grab a cup of your favorite beverage and sit in for the siege. Your goal is to sit there from about 10 in the morning until the early evening hours or later if you can. Try to schedule the visits to your local bookstore around a general payday, highlighting the time around school starting, or the beginning of summer. These are the two times where book sales are higher. People who have to come into the bookstore for a school book are most likely to fall for that impulse buy, and summer vacation brings all types of grandiose ideas of how much reading the average reader can catch up on.

Take note of who is perusing the same aisles. If you can, try to figure out what made them choose the book they did. This is the start of your market research. Make notes of colors they are attracted to, did they open the book and read the first page, or read from the middle? Did they have a list or seem to have a direction, or are they wandering aimlessly? Do they choose and clear the store in less than 30 minutes (the impulse buy), or do they wander picking up books and putting them down, only to maybe go back again (the real way to buy books)? With the buyers who intrigue you the most, strike up a conversation. Do not talk about your book, the interest is in them and how they buy, find out how they chose the book in their arms, you can start by asking if the author is any good. You will find long conversations and tons of great information will be flowing giving you an insight as to how people think when they are being parted from their dollars. Always carry a notebook with you. You will be amazed at the information you get just talking to people and you are always ready to write it down so you don't forget it.

30

Bookstore Visit 1

Name of Book Store: _____

Address: _____

_____

Date: _____

Time: _____

Section: _____

My favorite drink for today: _____

Keep track of the number of people who pick up a book and then look at:

31

Covers First: _____

Interior First: _____

Beg. of Book: _____

Middle of Book: _____

End of Book: _____

Back Cover: _____

Notes

_____

_____

_____

_____

_____

More Notes

Bookstore Visit 2

Name of Book Store: ⸺⸺⸺⸺⸺⸺⸺⸺⸺

Address: ⸺⸺⸺⸺⸺⸺⸺⸺⸺

⸺⸺⸺⸺⸺⸺⸺⸺⸺

Date: ⸺⸺⸺⸺⸺⸺⸺⸺

Time: ⸺⸺⸺⸺⸺⸺⸺⸺

Section: ⸺⸺⸺⸺⸺⸺⸺⸺⸺

My favorite drink for today: ⸺⸺⸺⸺⸺⸺⸺

Keep track of the number of people who pick up a book and then look at:

Covers First: ⸺⸺⸺⸺⸺⸺⸺⸺

Interior First: ⸺⸺⸺⸺⸺⸺⸺⸺

Beg. of Book: ⸺⸺⸺⸺⸺⸺⸺⸺

Middle of Book: ⸺⸺⸺⸺⸺⸺⸺⸺

End of Book: ⸺⸺⸺⸺⸺⸺⸺⸺

Back Cover: ⸺⸺⸺⸺⸺⸺⸺⸺

Notes

⸺⸺⸺⸺⸺⸺⸺⸺⸺⸺⸺⸺

⸺⸺⸺⸺⸺⸺⸺⸺⸺⸺⸺⸺

⸺⸺⸺⸺⸺⸺⸺⸺⸺⸺⸺⸺

⸺⸺⸺⸺⸺⸺⸺⸺⸺⸺⸺⸺

⸺⸺⸺⸺⸺⸺⸺⸺⸺⸺⸺⸺

⸺⸺⸺⸺⸺⸺⸺⸺⸺⸺⸺⸺

More Notes

Bookstore Visit 3

Name of Book Store: _____

Address: _____
_____

Date: _____

Time: _____

Section: _____

My favorite drink for today: _____

Keep track of the number of people who pick up a book and then look at:

Covers First: _____

Interior First: _____

Beg. of Book: _____

Middle of Book: _____

End of Book: _____

Back Cover: _____

Notes

_____
_____
_____
_____
_____
_____

More Notes

Bookstore Visit 4

Name of Book Store: ————————————————————————

Address: ————————————————————————

————————————————————————

Date: ————————————————————————

Time: ————————————————————————

Section: ————————————————————————

My favorite drink for today: ————————————————

Keep track of the number of people who pick up a book and then look at:

Covers First: ————————————————————————

Interior First: ————————————————————————

Beg. of Book: ————————————————————————

Middle of Book: ————————————————————————

End of Book: ————————————————————————

Back Cover: ————————————————————————

Notes

————————————————————————

————————————————————————

————————————————————————

————————————————————————

————————————————————————

More Notes

Bookstore Visit 5

Name of Book Store: ————————————————

Address: ————————————————

————————————————

Date: ————————————————

Time: ————————————————

Section: ————————————————

My favorite drink for today: ————————————————

Keep track of the number of people who pick up a book and then look at:

Covers First: ————————————————

Interior First: ————————————————

Beg. of Book: ————————————————

Middle of Book: ————————————————

End of Book: ————————————————

Back Cover: ————————————————

Notes

————————————————

————————————————

————————————————

————————————————

————————————————

More Notes

40

Pick 5 authors in your genre, who are displayed near where you can picture your book being displayed. Look at the end caps, the books laying on the tables as you walked into the store, and those books featured as new releases, or employee picks. These books are your competition.

Title: _____

Genre: _____

ISBN: _____

Author: _____

Price (include all countries): _____

Publication date (Street date): _____

Series: _____

Short description of how your book is different: **41**

_____

_____

_____

_____

_____

_____

List 3 things that attracted you to this title:

_____

_____

_____

List 3 things that you do not like about this title:

_____

_____

_____

In your genre:

Title: _____

Genre: _____

    ISBN: _____

    Author: _____

    Price (include all countries): _____

    Publication date (Street date): _____

    Series: _____

Short description of how your book is different:

_____

42 _____

_____

_____

_____

_____

List 3 things that attracted you to this title:

_____

_____

_____

List 3 things that you do not like about this title:

_____

_____

_____

In your genre:

Title: _____

Genre: _____

    ISBN: _____

    Author: _____

    Price (include all countries): _____

    Publication date (Street date): _____

    Series: _____

Short description of how your book is different:

_____

_____ 43

_____

_____

_____

_____

List 3 things that attracted you to this title:

_____

_____

_____

List 3 things that you do not like about this title:

_____

_____

_____

In your genre:

Title: _____

Genre: _____

ISBN: _____

Author: _____

Price (include all countries): _____

Publication date (Street date): _____

Series: _____

Short description of how your book is different:

_____

44 _____

_____

_____

_____

_____

List 3 things that attracted you to this title:

_____

_____

_____

List 3 things that you do not like about this title:

_____

_____

_____

In your genre:

Title: _____

Genre: _____

ISBN: _____

Author: _____

Price (include all countries): _____

Publication date (Street date): _____

Series: _____

Short description of how your book is different:

_____

_____ **45**

_____

_____

_____

_____

List 3 things that attracted you to this title:

_____

_____

_____

List 3 things that you do not like about this title:

_____

_____

_____

Remembering that readers read a variety of genres and levels, try to look at new markets that your book may relate to. Pick 5 authors who are not in your genre displayed no where near where you can picture your book being displayed. Look at the end caps, the books laying on the tables as you walked into the store, and those books featured as new releases, or employee picks. These books are also your competition.

Title: _____

Genre: _____

ISBN: _____

Author: _____

Price (include all countries): _____

Publication date (Street date): _____

Series: _____

46   Short description of how your book is the same:

_____

_____

_____

_____

_____

_____

List 3 things that attracted you to this title:

_____

_____

_____

List 3 things that you do not like about this title:

_____

_____

_____

Not in your genre:

Title: _____

Genre: _____

ISBN: _____

Author: _____

Price (include all countries): _____

Publication date (Street date): _____

Series: _____

Short description of how your book is the same:

_____

_____ 47

_____

_____

_____

_____

List 3 things that attracted you to this title:

_____

_____

_____

List 3 things that you do not like about this title:

_____

_____

_____

Not in your genre:

Title: _____

Genre: _____

    ISBN: _____

    Author: _____

    Price (include all countries): _____

    Publication date (Street date): _____

    Series: _____

Short description of how your book is the same:

_____

48 _____

_____

_____

_____

List 3 things that attracted you to this title:

_____

_____

_____

List 3 things that you do not like about this title:

_____

_____

_____

Not in your genre:

Title: _____

Genre: _____

    ISBN: _____

    Author: _____

    Price (include all countries): _____

    Publication date (Street date): _____

    Series: _____

Short description of how your book is the same:

_____

_____   **49**

_____

_____

_____

_____

List 3 things that attracted you to this title:

_____

_____

_____

List 3 things that you do not like about this title:

_____

_____

_____

Not in your genre:

Title: _____

Genre: _____

    ISBN: _____

    Author: _____

    Price (include all countries): _____

    Publication date (Street date): _____

    Series: _____

Short description of how your book is the same:

50
_____
_____
_____
_____
_____

List 3 things that attracted you to this title:

_____
_____
_____

List 3 things that you do not like about this title:

_____
_____
_____

E-Books

The internet has changed the world! Everything from how we communicate to how we search for places to vacation, is now at our fingertips. In addition, there is a whole new generation of clients that now own Kindles™, Nooks™ and Nobos™ (and the new e-reader products that will be available soon and in the future), granting access to purchase your book instantly! Plus anyone who owns a computer, laptop, netbook, or tablet can download a free Kindle reader and read in the comfort of their home sitting in their recliner. Let's not forget that everything runs around on a cloud now too. This is a market you can't afford not to consider in your marketing plan because if you do not, you will lose a multitude of potential sales.

Market Viability becomes shorter as technology grows.

Speaking as a professional who utilizes the PC and a Kindle, I can tell you it is easy, convenient and fast, less expensive and can be accessed 24 hours a day. In the current economy, how long do you think it will take for the people you want to purchase your book to take advantage of this medium? May I take a moment to be selfish and ask, "How many sales might this bring?" Besides, didn't you write your book on a computer in the first place? Are you reading this book in the handy, dandy electronic format?

51

With the introduction of tablets into the market, we can read any place, any time, and have access to thousands of free and low priced books. Overhead and production costs are virtually non existent with these new technologies. Textbooks have been in electronic format for years, but they were difficult and cumbersome. The newest technologies allow these textbooks to be more accessible, easier to use and instantly available. This new technology has tons of health benefits: Our children's backs will not be deformed by carrying around a hundred pounds of books in a back pack flung across their shoulders; the devices are so small, light and hold so much information that we don't have to pay an extra baggage fee just for our summer reading books that we take on vacation; and our stress level goes down as our guilt for spending thirty bucks on a single book is a thing of the past. Now if only our eating habits were so easily managed.

Now tracking sales and how people buy electronically is going to be difficult at best. There isn't this instant spy camera that can allow you to peek over their shoulders at 2 in the morning, because they have to find something new to read. There are two ways to tackle this type of research. The first is the easiest, do the research for yourself. Make a list of people you would buy books for, make it a vast list with many differing styles, education levels, desires, interests and reading levels. Now it is time to fill out these forms again. **Pay attention** the first five are in your genre, and the last five are out of your genre.

In your genre:

Title: _____

Genre: _____

    ISBN: _____

    Author: _____

    Price (include all countries): _____

    Publication date (Street date): _____

    Series: _____

Short description of how your book is different:

_____

_____

_____

_____

_____

List 3 things that attracted you to this title:

_____

_____

_____

List 3 things that you do not like about this title:

_____

_____

_____

In your genre:

Title: _____

Genre: _____

ISBN: _____

Author: _____

Price (include all countries): _____

Publication date (Street date): _____

Series: _____

Short description of how your book is different:

_____
_____

53

_____
_____
_____
_____

List 3 things that attracted you to this title:

_____
_____
_____

List 3 things that you do not like about this title:

_____
_____
_____

In your genre:

Title: _____

Genre: _____

ISBN: _____

Author: _____

Price (include all countries): _____

Publication date (Street date): _____

Series: _____

Short description of how your book is different:

_____

_____

_____

_____

_____

List 3 things that attracted you to this title:

_____

_____

_____

List 3 things that you do not like about this title:

_____

_____

_____

In your genre:

Title: _____

Genre: _____

ISBN: _____

Author: _____

Price (include all countries): _____

Publication date (Street date): _____

Series: _____

Short description of how your book is different:

_____

_____ **55**

_____

_____

_____

_____

List 3 things that attracted you to this title:

_____

_____

_____

List 3 things that you do not like about this title:

_____

_____

_____

In your genre:

Title: _____

Genre: _____

ISBN: _____

Author: _____

Price (include all countries): _____

Publication date (Street date): _____

Series: _____

Short description of how your book is different:

_____

_____

_____

_____

_____

List 3 things that attracted you to this title:

_____

_____

_____

List 3 things that you do not like about this title:

_____

_____

_____

Not in your genre:

Title: _____

Genre: _____

ISBN: _____

Author: _____

Price (include all countries): _____

Publication date (Street date): _____

Series: _____

Short description of how your book is the same:

_____

_____ **57**

_____

_____

_____

List 3 things that attracted you to this title:

_____

_____

List 3 things that you do not like about this title:

_____

_____

_____

Not in your genre:

Title: _____

Genre: _____

ISBN: _____

Author: _____

Price (include all countries): _____

Publication date (Street date): _____

Series: _____

Short description of how your book is the same:

_____

_____

_____

_____

_____

_____

List 3 things that attracted you to this title:

_____

_____

_____

List 3 things that you do not like about this title:

_____

_____

_____

Not in your genre:

Title: _____

Genre: _____

ISBN: _____

Author: _____

Price (include all countries): _____

Publication date (Street date): _____

Series: _____

Short description of how your book is the same:

_____

_____ **59**

_____

_____

_____

List 3 things that attracted you to this title:

_____

_____

List 3 things that you do not like about this title:

_____

_____

_____

Not in your genre:

Title: _____

Genre: _____

    ISBN: _____

    Author: _____

    Price (include all countries): _____

    Publication date (Street date): _____

    Series: _____

Short description of how your book is the same:

_____

60 _____

_____

_____

_____

_____

List 3 things that attracted you to this title:

_____

_____

_____

List 3 things that you do not like about this title:

_____

_____

_____

Not in your genre:

Title: _____

Genre: _____

    ISBN: _____

    Author: _____

    Price (include all countries): _____

    Publication date (Street date): _____

    Series: _____

Short description of how your book is the same:

_____
_____
_____
_____
_____

List 3 things that attracted you to this title:

_____
_____

List 3 things that you do not like about this title:

_____
_____
_____

The second requires some social detective work. Go to lunch with your friends, interview them and find out how they buy electronic books. Make a list of at least ten different ways that they make their final decisions. Automatically throw out the following:

1. It is an author I normally read.
2. Someone recommended the book.
3. Why of course it is yours so I bought it.

We know that readers tend to buy authors they like and will read them until they quit writing (for the epochally optimistic), or the author starts producing total crap, (for the true connoisseurs). We also know that 85% of all readers choose new authors based on a friend's recommendation. As a new author, you want to know how they choose a book they have never heard of, or seen before. That is the question you need the most variety of answers for. There is no format for this type of research and it always results in a long overdue coffee or dinner with a friend you have been meaning to get in touch with. Take a notebook and just have a nice relaxed visit. It may be the last one you get for a while.

Creating A Marketing Plan

A marketing plan is a clearly defined plan that moves you from goal to goal, pushing your book to the next level. It is usually written on the thinnest paper you can find, with an overwhelming amount of eraser marks, strike outs and arrows, redirecting every idea. What I am trying to say is that your marketing plan is an idea, a very loosely organized plan that is adaptable to life interfering. Please take a moment and breathe here.

It is very important to know that this process can take over your entire life. You get so wrapped up in every nuance, of every detail; that you will be lost to any sort of rational thought that doesn't encompass you, your book and your immediate responsibilities and priorities. The rest of life interferes and you come up for air, looking at everyone as if they have grown a third eye, or an extra head and wondering how you can use it. There are some real life catastrophes and not making your sales quota or writing deadline, do not qualify. Almost every author I have worked with over the past 15 years has had something pop into their world that they just couldn't ignore: The loss of a job, a new baby, a hurricane, or cancer in not only one sibling but two.

63

Goal setting is a system. A way to challenge your inner self and create a more positive and favorable world for you. Goal setting is the engine that keeps the mind occupied, the soul alive and moves you to the next level of excellence. Accomplished every day, goals add up over time. When calculating the amount of goals I have personally and professionally set and completed I find that

Accomplished every day, goals add up over time.

I have lost count. The importance of the exercise is to realize your goals and then make steps to complete the small tasks for the big mountain. Personally, I have accomplished the goals that are common for any mother or wife. I have a successful marriage with over twenty years behind us and many more in front. We have two wonderful young men. Both equally responsible for their age and always going above and beyond the call. As a family that alone covers the one million and one goals I have set so far.

As a professional, I have had several occupations. From manager of a company in Hawaii to entrepreneur of the company I run now. I see goals that are set and achieved daily, not only by myself but by the entire team with whom I have the pleasure of working. I see a completed manuscript that someone thought they couldn't finish, and in reality, they could. I see the look on someone's face as they hold their book for the first time, as they complete their first book signing and when a fan is over the top for them. I watch as colleagues dealt the worst hand possible, rise to the occasion and achieve their dreams for the next level of professional success. Their goals accomplished, and a new challenge already facing them.

When creating your goals you need to analyze your market, recognize your competition, and consider the marketing strategies of others in your genre. Carefully allow for life to weave in and out, keeping you on your toes and fresh for the next hurdle.

Before you get started in this section, make sure you have done research in at least three different book stores. The second step to a marketing plan is your competition. This is the fun part, in your pajamas with your beverage of choice. From your list of twenty titles from the previous section it is time to do some online research.

Choose three different authors from your twenty titles:

Choose one very established author. An established author is an author who even a non-reader would recognize such as: Nora Roberts, Tom Clancy, Steven King, Dean Koontz, James Patterson, etc. These are authors with a minimum of fifty published books, and over a fourth have been on the best sellers lists and have won some award.

Your second author is a semi-established or known author. This is an author who readers may know such as: Patricia Briggs, Robin Hobb or Nicholas Sparks . They have between twenty and fifty published titles. These are also award winners, but either don't have the best selling titles, or are not producing more than one title every year, or every other year.

Your third author is a new author. This author has less than 20 books, looking more toward the five to 15 range of books published. This means they have been at it for a while, have enough peer review to have survived the literary vetting process, and are the perfect place you want to be in the next three to five years. Authors that fit this area are: Lauren Kate, Melissa Marr, or Stephenie Meyers.

My Competition – (Established)

Name of Author: _____

Web Address: _____
_____

Date: _____

Time: _____

List three things you like about the appearance of the web site.

_____

_____

_____

List three things you don't like about the appearance of the web site.

_____

_____

_____

List one marketing tool you hadn't thought of.

_____

_____

_____

More Notes

66

My Competition – (Established)

Name of Author: ————————————————————

Blog Address: ————————————————————

————————————————————

Date: ————————————————————

Time: ————————————————————

List three things you like about the appearance of the blog.

————————————————————

————————————————————

————————————————————

List three things you don't like about the appearance of the blog.

————————————————————

————————————————————

————————————————————

List one marketing tool you hadn't thought of.

————————————————————

————————————————————

————————————————————

More Notes

My Competition – (Established)

Name of Author: _____

Fantastic Fiction Address: _____

_____

Date: _____

Time: _____

List three things you like about the appearance of the author page.

_____

_____

List three things you don't like about the appearance of the author page.

_____

_____

List one marketing tool you hadn't thought of.

_____

_____

More Notes

My Competition – (Established)

Name of Author: _____

Facebook® Address: _____

_____

Date: _____

Time: _____

List three things you like about the appearance of the Facebook® page.

_____

_____

_____

List three things you don't like about the appearance of the Facebook® page.

_____

_____

_____

List one marketing tool you hadn't thought of.

_____

_____

_____

More Notes

My Competition – (Established)

Name of Author: _____

Amazon® Author Page Address: _____

Date: _____

Time: _____

List three things you like about the appearance of the Amazon® Author Page.

_____

_____

_____

73

List three things you don't like about the appearance of the Amazon® Author Page.

_____

_____

_____

List one marketing tool you hadn't thought of.

_____

_____

_____

More Notes

My Competition – (Semi Established)

Name of Author: _____

Web Address: _____
_____

Date: _____

Time: _____

List three things you like about the appearance of the web site.

_____

_____

_____

List three things you don't like about the appearance of the web site.

_____

_____

_____

List one marketing tool you hadn't thought of.

_____

_____

_____

More Notes

My Competition – (Semi Established)

Name of Author: _____

Blog Address: _____

_____

Date: _____

Time: _____

List three things you like about the appearance of the blog.

_____

_____

_____

List three things you don't like about the appearance of the blog.

_____

_____

_____

List one marketing tool you hadn't thought of.

_____

_____

_____

More Notes

78

My Competition – (Semi Established)

Name of Author: _____

Fantastic Fiction Address: _____

_____

Date: _____

Time: _____

List three things you like about the appearance of the author page.

_____

_____

_____ 79

List three things you don't like about the appearance of the author page.

_____

_____

_____

List one marketing tool you hadn't thought of.

_____

_____

_____

More Notes

My Competition – (Semi Established)

Name of Author: _____

Facebook® Address: _____

_____

Date: _____

Time: _____

List three things you like about the appearance of the Facebook® page.

_____

_____

_____

List three things you don't like about the appearance of the Facebook® page.

_____

_____

_____

List one marketing tool you hadn't thought of.

_____

_____

_____

More Notes

My Competition – (Semi Established)

Name of Author: _____

Amazon® Author page Address: _____
_____

Date: _____

Time: _____

List three things you like about the appearance of the Amazon® Author page.

_____

_____

_____

83

List three things you don't like about the appearance of the Amazon® Author page.

_____

_____

_____

List one marketing tool you hadn't thought of.

_____

_____

_____

More Notes

My Competition – (New Author)

Name of Author: _____

Web Address: _____
_____

Date: _____

Time: _____

List three things you like about the appearance of the web site.

_____

_____

_____

List three things you don't like about the appearance of the web site.

_____

_____

_____

List one marketing tool you hadn't thought of.

_____

_____

_____

More Notes

My Competition – (New Author)

Name of Author: _____

Blog Address: _____
_____

Date: _____

Time: _____

List three things you like about the appearance of the blog.

_____
_____
_____

List three things you don't like about the appearance of the blog.

_____
_____
_____

List one marketing tool you hadn't thought of.

_____
_____
_____

More Notes

My Competition – (New Author)

Name of Author: _____

Fantastic Fiction Address: _____
_____

Date: _____

Time: _____

List three things you like about the appearance of the author page.

_____
_____
_____

List three things you don't like about the appearance of the author page.

_____
_____
_____

List one marketing tool you hadn't thought of.

_____
_____
_____

More Notes

My Competition – (New Author)

Name of Author: _____

Facebook® Address: _____
_____

Date: _____

Time: _____

List three things you like about the appearance of the Facebook® page.

_____

_____

_____

List three things you don't like about the appearance of the Facebook® page.

_____

_____

_____

List one marketing tool you hadn't thought of

_____

_____

_____

More Notes

My Competition– (New Author)

Name of Author: _____

Amazon® Author Page Address: _____
_____

Date: _____

Time: _____

List three things you like about the appearance of the Amazon® Author page.

_____

_____

93

_____

List three things you don't like about the appearance of the Amazon® Author page.

_____

_____

_____

List one marketing tool you hadn't thought of.

_____

_____

_____

More Notes

CHAPTER THREE: TIME BUDGET VERSUS MONEY BUDGET

Now that you have explored your goals you need to consider time management. You need to use your time wisely and work smarter not harder. One of the misnomers of working smart is that you can do just as much in half the time. If that was the case then everyone in this business would be a best seller. The truth is working smart means just making the best of your time. There are two portions of time management. The first is choosing which investment (time and/or money) will give you the greatest reward in the long term, and organizing your time in the way that best supports your attack strategy.

Choosing Investments – Time.

Some investments will require continual work. Things that require time or money continually are ones that you need to consider carefully. They include but are not limited to: Press packages, web sites, postcards, blogs and flyers. One option for maintaining these important marketing devices is a continuing education class at your local community college. A relatively small investment of money and time and you can learn how to create a high quality product at an affordable monetary investment (without hiring others) that will benefit you in the long run. This is a great example of putting your time and money into an activity that will allow you to control your presentation, have it in a timely manner and make last minute changes that look professional and planned.

This is a Business!

So, start by thinking of two things you want to focus on during each quarter of the year. As you work through the quarter, focusing on what you need to accomplish you will find that by the end of the quarter you have more time that you expected. Startup takes a lot longer than maintenance, so start one new thing every quarter and then just maintain them. By the time you are through your first year you will have created a system that is integrated with the rest of your life. Your task list will become more diverse and targeted as you figure out where your time investments are paying off.

Choosing Investments – Money

My favorite four letter word is BUDGET. Yes, despite how many times you count it, I classify it as a four letter word. A budget is something none of us want to worry about. We prefer to collect adulation from all our adoring fans and not think too hard about money. However, this is a business so you need to determine the average number of sales calls you will need to make per sale, the average dollar size per sale, and the average dollar size per vendor. The larger the dollar size, the fewer calls or the more money.

When thinking budget, remember this is a BUSINESS and you must treat it as such. Keep track of everything. You will need proof of what you've spent as an owner. No one is just going to take your word for it. You will need to include everything from meals to mileage, and things you never thought might apply.

Always dream and gauge bigger than you think.

Define and organize your budget. You don't have to have a multi-million dollar budget to be successful, although in all honesty, it would make it a lot easier. What you need is a carefully defined budget. Any amount is better than nothing. If you have $50 to spend for the month, that can work. Your job will be to discover how you can get $500 worth of investments out of that $50. Here your imagination and creativity can really be put to good use. Use your market research to find ways of doing things out of the box. Remember things that you do for free can result in free press. Volunteering and donations can be good for everyone!

There are several items that most authors don't budget for that can add up, undermining their best efforts. Budget your time! Keep careful track of your time and find out per unit how much you are making per hour. It will help you find where the greatest action is resulting in the highest profit, and that in turn will help your work smarter. I use a standard time card and time clock to keep track of my time on a project. It isn't the most accurate, and honestly, I forget to do it sometimes, but I get better and better every day and can see where my efforts are returned.

96

Budget for mailing expenses! You remember the stamps and the priority mail, but do you remember the cost of the envelope, the cost of the piece of paper or the ink that you use. These are hidden costs that can add up fast. Using things around your home office that you have already purchased or are part of living and working environment will make that $50 go a lot further. Don't forget they are still an expense and as you use them they will have to be replaced. The internet

Time Investment	Monthly Reoccurring	Quarterly Reoccurring	Yearly Reoccurring
Advertising/Promotions	Stamps	Manila folders	Tax
Research	Delivery Expenses (FedEX, UPS,	Copier Rental & Supplies	Staff
Charity	USPS)	Interest Charges	Long Term File Storage
Business Cards	Ink Cartridges	Paper Clips	Computer Hardware
Mailings	Paper	Billboards	Subscriptions
Advertising (newsp/tv/radio)	Employees/Temps.	Pencils/Pens	Trade Publications
Promotional Brochures	Mileage	Govt. Taxes & Remitns	Subscriptions
Publicity/Marketing	Printing Services	Binders	Professional Assoc. Fees
Web site Design	Phone Fees	Shredding & Disposal Svcs.	Domain Names
Office Cleaning	Credit Card Charges	On Line Workshop Fees	Web site hosting
Postcards	Internet	Valet Service	
Signs	Rent	Staples	
Start Up Expenses	Telephone Ans. Svcs.	College Class Fees	
LLC Formation	Entertainment Fees	Conference Fees	
Licenses	Food/Beverages	Airline Tickets	
Ins.(Liability/Casualty)		Hotel Fees	
Desk/Other Office Furniture		Taxi	
Office Supplies		Audio/Visual Services	
Computer		Charity Event Expenses	
Computer Software		Bus Sides	
Basic PA/Podium		Sponsorships	
XGA Data/Video Projector			

service, electricity, water and (most importantly for me) coffee, all add up and contribute to that bottom line. Even if you would have had to pay that bill anyway, it doesn't undermine the importance of the money spent on those items for that time you are working on your promotions. In a separate office on in the middle of your living room, these costs should still be considered in your bottom line. Don't fret or worry over the details around each of the times you need to track, just make it part of your everyday routine. You need to know where your $50 is going and you need to know where your time is the most productive. Knowing gives you two important items: seeing that your effort is producing results, and working smart.

Remember that what works best for others may not work best for you. So how do you know what works? Do what the others suggest. It did work for them. Also, keep track of what you do. Your success will be a combination of what they did, what you do, and what others do for you.

When constructing your monetary budget always dream and gauge bigger than you think. Things are always going to cost less in some months, and more in others. Setting your budget at the higher value for every month gives you more to play with, most of the time.

Chapter Four: Social Networking
(Time Budget)

Social networking is one of the most effective tools for reaching a wide market. This chapter is not how to set up and integrate your social network, but how to use portions of the various attributes for marketing your books and then marketing yourself as a professional author or speaker. There are numerous tutorials on how to do everything suggested here

It will take time to find what works best for you. Remember what you are going to read is only my opinion and what works for me. It may not and is not expected to work as well for everyone. So research, knowledge and experience on all of the available venues is really the best suggestion I can give you. Investigate what you have at your fingertips.

Facebook®, YouTube®, MySpace®, Twitter®, blogging, and RSS Feeds are all terms that are used in our everyday computing world. It is all free and it is all a time sink. You can find that you spend hours on any of these various aspects of the virtual market and not be accomplishing anything. I figured out what worked for me by spending hours in this time sink and keeping track of the return for the time invested, to find out what really was worth my efforts.

The more book buyers see you networking the more apt they are to support your book signing.

These applications are trusted sites that are very safe. You do not purchase anything through them, so no one can get your financial information. You are only required to put in the bare minimum of information as required by congressional law, minimizing the ability of someone to steal your identity. You are notified through an anonymous third party application, one that you cannot reply to or trace without a great deal of effort. Now does this guarantee your safety? No way! Anything you access on the internet is available to those that really want to put in the effort, but these applications have done everything they can to protect your usage information with all the technology they have currently available.

In addition there are control measures available on most of them that you can set which let as much or as little of your personal information as you wish to become available to the public. And I do mean, to the public, because you MUST remember that this is the internet. At the very minimum, your "friends" can view everything you allow. The best way to make sure you only divulge what you're comfortable with is to remember that whatever you put out there can and will become available to anyone and everyone. So if you don't wish your personal business to become record, don't put it out there.

Which sites should you use? Try them all! Consider two things when deciding which is best for you: The tools associated with each of the applications, and the audiences.

MySpace® is primarily used for the mass marketing group. Inhabited mainly by younger groups who are attracted to the pretty pictures and clutter you find on MySpace®, they are also the number one consumer for all things Pop Culture; music, movies, clothing, comics. If you are writing young adult or early adulthood fiction then this is the place you want to market. It worked for Taylor Swift and Lady Gaga.

Facebook® is for those who are a little older and less prone to be attracted to the flashing lights and colorful rainbows that appear on MySpace® It is a place where you can talk about your book and even ask people to "like" your page, but if you choose to do that I would suggest that you make sure that your "friends" know who you are as a person first. People will respond better to someone who has participated and/or commented on what is going on with them than to someone who all of a sudden wants them to do something or buy something or even "like" something when they have never seen any type of posting from them.

LinkedIn® is for the professional side of you. Although others may care about your book, they care more about what they can pay you to do to help them advance their careers. This is perfect for the professional or money making part of what you do. LinkedIn® is not about selling units of your book, but about selling yourself as someone who can contribute and offer expertise to an individual group, corporation or institution.

Google+® is our one stop shopping mall. An easy to use, interactive representation of all of the social networks listed above. Google® has introduced the concept of circles, which Facebook® currently utilizes with it's current update. But Google's® are easier to use and allow you to direct your marketing and information to a specific source. It also allows you to post your latest hot date without letting the professional world see it. If you have several products with several different audiences.. Goodgle® circles allow you to target those audiences with a click. It also connects and utilizes all the Google® apps, such as calendars, e-mails , blogs, micro blogging and the social network. It encapsulates Twitter's® waterfall style distribution of information from your circle to anyone within your circle and then anyone in their circle cascading to reach a targeted market with the same interests with minimal research. Although Google® should not replace any other targeted social networking site it does streamline the process touching the entire Google® world.

> Note: My brother works for major a computer company building internet stuffs -yes stuffs is a technical term that can be applied generically - his reply to my questions on safety and the internet is, "If you want fail safe internet security, get off the internet and unplug your computer from the wall."

There are other types of social networking sites that focus specifically on a hobby or interest. You can find lists of them with a simple search of social networks on the web, from Academia.edu for the academics in your life, to Zooppa® for a social network for creative talents. Hey isn't that you? However, finding the right one for you will take research, which translates to time. You may need to use more than one or two networking sites in order to accomplish your goals, but I would suggest you limit your time on each one unless you can afford to spend hours on this project and no other.

They are all equally easy to use, and have all of the same general features and securities for their users. Their spam rules and regulations are generally the same as well as their privacy protocols. Their audiences are different and you need to make sure that your copy and marketing information fits. The same rules you apply to how you use your social networks applies to the rest of this chapter. Make sure you check out each of them thoroughly along with the rules, features and securities before you decide which is best for you. Then ask yourself the same set of questions when establishing your blogs, RSS feeds, YouTube® videos, or your author pages on various sites such as Amazon®. Remember, there are a minimum of three hundred plus major, active social networking sites, are added, modified and changed on a daily basis. Continually monitor your time sinks and adjust for the best bang.

Marketing Persona

The purpose of the marketing persona is to market your book, to find the perfect set of words to get someone to part from their dollar and give it to you. So the first thing you need to do is find a theme. Make your theme interesting or useful, and make sure it is entertaining. If your readers start finding your copy to be boring or tedious they are going to become uninterested and fall from your following.

Describe how you want people to see you as an author.

101

_____

_____

_____

_____

If you are writing a fictional book and your product is your story, then your page should be about things that your main characters are doing or even have the copy in the voice of your character. If you have multiple characters that chat at you all the time, then create a page for the group and have them all talk at the same time. Have fun with it. Tell mini stories about the everyday life of the characters, introduce new ideas and encourage feedback from your fans.

Describe how you want people to see your characters outside of the book.

_____

_____

_____

_____

_____

Get the fans involved and make them feel as if they are living and breathing with the characters as much as you do. I find Facebook®'s page or group pages are great as you get more followers and members, then a simple post works to reach everyone who already has shown an interest in your product. Creating a page or group is easy to do through Facebook®, and your followers really don't expect you to post often, at most twice a week.

Describe some of the postings that you would like to see your fans make on your fan page.

_____

_____

_____

_____

_____

The Facebook® group page announcements not only go to your fans' Facebook® e-mail but are usually forwarded to their personal e-mail making sure that your message will at least be glanced at. It also falls into the safety parameters of solicited e-mails. Your messages will not go to the spam folder automatically because it is coming from a source that the receiver has already authorized.

As Facebook® has these features so do the other social networks. Look at MySpace®'s area to setup and promote a single book, character or image. You can also connect to all the other blogging mechanisms available. Remember best selling fictional authors are pop culture, so get onto MySpace® and use it. Especially for those young adult, tween and children's books!

Describe how you would like a 10 year old to view your book.

_____

_____

_____

_____

_____

Now we are all smart, and we accept and know that a majority of our money is not going to come from book sales, but from our public exposure, the conference fees people want to pay us because we are so successful, and our subsidiary rights, and all of this is based on our knowledge. Before you say "I really don't know that much," that is true, you don't. What you do know though is very focused, very detailed, and very much intriguing to about one percent of the population, at least on a slightly deeper level than just, "Hey, that plant is blue." LinkedIn® is the best and most professional of all the social networking sites. It requires a minimal set up and minimal maintenance except to pop in once a week to check on new contacts, or update your profile as needed. It is basically a clearing house for experts, of which you are now one.

A company has contacted you to present to their employees as a motivational speaker in sales. Describe your mission statement for the talk, and list five key points that you would like to be known for:

_____

_____

_____

_____

_____

Sales is an easy one, and if you are going to be successful in this business you need to understand how sales work, and how to acquire as many as you can. Sales fall into many categories within the realm of the book business. There are actual unit sales of your book and sales of your supporting information. The biggest sale, the most important sale, is selling yourself. Luckily with that you have several different products to pedal.

You have the author as an author, talking about the exploits of writing, the epic battles that were fought in your head and how you called your editor at two in the morning to complain about your characters talking to you, and she told you, "So go and talk back.," and then hung up. You have the professional you are before you added author to your personality list. Were you a real estate agent, an insurance broker, a housewife, a school teacher. Think of all the things you can talk about from that life, and how you can present to and educate the general public. You also now have a detailed,

You do this because you want it!

focused knowledge of the subject matter that loosely holds your stories together. If you are writing books that are very loosely connected to a religion and you did your research, you know more about that religion than most of the people who attend that church. How about an artist, or a city, or cooking, quilting, gardening, cleaning, or my all time favorite, making the perfect margarita? You are now an expert in all of these, knowing more than the average person, and you have a lot to share.

Now list at least ten other specific, focused subjects you can speak on and develop for workshops and presentations.

_____

_____

_____

_____

_____

_____

_____

_____

_____

_____

_____

Marketing Blogs

B logs and RSS feeds are one in the same. For your marketing pages for your books, blogs can be very helpful in keeping your fans interested between book releases. Think of a blog as a micro diary of the new and exciting happening in the life of your story line, characters, professional speaking or coaching career. Then you make it interactive by allowing your readers to comment and give you feedback about what they like or don't like. It may not change how you write your next book, but it may give you new information for subsequent writings, ways to improve your presentations, what works for your audiences and what doesn't, and what new trends readers are looking for. Blogs are no longer than about two-hundred-fifty words.

Your blog that is written in the voice of your character needs a subject that relates to your general reading audience. For this exercise we are going to use the subject of shoes. Specifically, the 2010 version of the Manolo Blahnik Leather Heart Sandal with ankle strap. Write what your main character would say about this find, in their voice. (Guys, whether you like shoes or not they are one of the items that sells books, so pick a stand and write about the shoe.)

There are several ideas for using blogs from the point of view of marketing your books. You are only limited by your imagination. Blogs can be used to try out new plot or story lines with your readers. They can also be used for your characters to have micro adventures in between books. A blog allows comments from your fan base not only about your story lines but also about your characters.

Write a conversation between your two main characters out walking around for a night on the town.

_____

_____

_____

_____

_____

_____

_____

_____

_____

Comments are very useful and helpful to a writer. Getting ideas and feedback allows your writing and story lines to be fresh, up to date and interactive. Remember that everyone has an opinion and that these opinions can be helpful, if not for your current project maybe for a subsequent one. Encouraging your readers to be involved in what you write allows them to be active and interested, resulting in more book sales.

Write what comments you would like to see about your shoe post.

_____

_____

_____

_____

_____

_____

_____

_____

_____

_____

Professional blogs

As a professional you have a specialty, you are an expert. Taking your interests and what you are promoting professionally, create a theme that is aimed at the audience you want to attract and open it up for comments. Your professional blog should be informative, creative, entertaining and helpful. Remember that when you are trying to get new clients to part with their dollars, that the more information you overwhelm them with the more they are going to value what you say. Remember that everyone can do it, if they have the mind, time and motivation to do it. Your job is to become so indispensable and make it so mired in details that the only person who can do the job is you.

The theme for your professional blog is very different and has a vastly different audience than your theme for your readers. Your professional blog is one that provides information on a specific topic that you have been doing in minutia. This can be anything from managing a schedule, and making stuff happen, to how to cook the perfect soufflé. The preparation and dedication will collect you an audience that will pay for your information. Individuals will buy the book or come and hear you speak because they feel as if they have an intimate relationship with you. As an author, an intimate relationship between your characters and your reading audience is an important networking tool that increases your reputation, your marketing persona and your bottom line.

106 Write a personal blog type memoir about the latest battle with your story line and who won. Remember do not give away any of the details, just a tantalizing bit that makes people want to buy the next installment.

_____

_____

_____

_____

_____

Write a tidbit of help from one of your expert selections from the previous entries. A hint, instruction, description or solution to a situation related to that expert status.

_____

_____

_____

_____

When looking for a blog engine, I prefer WordPress®. The single reason for this is my ability to create and schedule the postings of the blog. After spending the time to tweak my blog the way I like it, I am then able to spend an entire eight hours to write, edit, set up and schedule blogs for the entire quarter. Think of that one day every quarter where you can write short passages that are interconnected that will continually keep you in the search loops strictly because you post on a regular basis.

Micro Blogging

Micro blogging has been created and defined by Twitter®. It is making an announcement in one hundred forty characters or less. Using Twitter® has an amazing cascade effect in the number of people you reach with a single post. This cascading effect allows you to easily and exponentially expand the amount of people you reach in one blast. When you send a blast to one person it cascades and then through all their contacts as an overflow. You can easily reach a new audience and new marketing leads by using this application.

Writing copy for micro blogging is a real art. You have one hundred forty characters (including spaces and punctuation) to make your announcement. Within one hundred forty characters you have to be interesting and catchy. Someone who gets one hundred fifty notifications a day needs to find your posting interesting enough to follow up. To allow that follow up you need to include your web site information. That will take fifteen to twenty characters out of your one hundred forty. So be interesting and catchy with less. Since you will need to post frequently, you need to make sure **107** your postings are varied enough that they do not get boring.

Using Twitter® seems to be the greatest time sink with little or no way to track its effectiveness. That being the case I have found it best to "tweet" four or five times a day and engage with others. Once you decide how often to "tweet", pick a theme and follow. If you are "tweeting" four or five times a day, every day, then from your characters' point of view, get mired in the details of everyday living. Do "tweets" about a new recipe or the frustration and joy of shopping for the perfect little black dress or those shoes that your wife is going to make you wear on the cruise, and they have to be comfortable.

You can't schedule "tweets" through the Twitter® interface but you can e-mail them. By using the delayed sending commands in most e-mail programs you can schedule "tweets" en masse. Since you are using the characters and their acts of minutia to entertain the masses, then my suggestion is that you sit down and write them all at the same time. Remember these are tidbits, that are being "tweeted" as your character would be "discovering" them on their own. Try taking some of your entertaining and embarrassing moments and incorporate them from your characters' perspectives and use them for your "tweets". Have fun with it and allow yourself to poke some fun at yourself with this process.

Video Blogging

YouTube® is the leading video medium in the world right now. Used effectively it has launched one of the newest and inspirational stories for a young country singer. So how do you use it when promoting your characters? It is a great place to post commercials that either link back to your books or a short story you have running on your web site. You can use it to post interviews with you as an author about your books, someone reading your book, or even just you talking about the process of writing the story and how it has changed and affected your life.

Write a script or description of a video blog you would like to see about your book.

Chapter Five: Your Marketing And Publicity Package
(Time and Money)

Your marketing and publicity package is the professional industry's first glance at you. What does that mean? It is the first thing potential buyers and managers will see. It is very important. It will require time, tweaking and patience to produce a perfect professional package. There are several ways that you can produce this package. Hire someone. This is the easiest but most expensive. You will still have to put in the time, accomplish the tweaking and hold on to your patience to create the perfect package, but someone else is doing the work. The drawback is that you are held hostage to their schedule. If you need it on the run, give it up or expect to pay out the nose for the immediate change. Remember that getting your information to the prospective buyer is time sensitive, and it must be personalized. Therefore, have a slush fund just for the purpose of paying to have it done on the fly.

Instant gratification does not exist.

Do it yourself. As long as you are willing to learn, there is no need for you to hire someone to do everything. You can do it yourself, update when you need to (which is frequently), and produce it as you need it. Try your local community college continuing education department for classes offered that might make this task easier. Classes in using current web programs (so that you can maintain your own web site or blog) or current graphics programs (so that you can design eye appealing packages) may help you. Classes may be weeks of invested time, and are less monetary investment than hiring someone, but you may save yourself tons of time, frustration and money in the end.

Do some yourself and hire out the rest. Perhaps you are good with (or can learn) some of the skills needed (for example, web page creation), but not with others (such as art work). You can always hire out parts of the work. To save money, try finding an art student or someone with experience in a graphics program to assist you with layout and design. There are several layout and design artists out there who are new and starting out and would love the business. Run a help wanted ad or contact the local art guild to see if anyone in your area is interested. The type of layout and design artist you want is one who does business cards, brochures and maybe a little fancy artwork. You do not need a full blown artist. Also, remember that this is considered "work for hire" and you should be free to use anything they create without restriction.

Questions to ask a layout and design artist are:

    a. Can you produce everything in .tiff format?
    b. Can you upload to a printing company?
    c. Do you take payments?
    d. Can I see a copy of your contract?

Contents of the Package

Publicity packages have been the same for years. They must be easy to read, easy to follow, and easy for the media and book buyers to find information in. They need to be attractive, entertaining, informative, and yet still meet and contain all the information necessary for the media to do advertising for you. Below is a list of the basic marketing material you will need to create or have created, and a short description of what each one should include.

Chapter by Chapter Synopsis: This is the life line to selling your book and it must be done with precise care. A brief but detailed chapter by chapter description keeping it within the eight to ten page guideline. Each chapter should have its own three to five sentence paragraph. Do not go over ten pages for the entire synopsis. If you do you give away too much information. Additionally, professional book buyers and coordinators do not want to read a long synopsis. They do not have the time. The purpose is to describe, intrigue and hook the buyer into wanting to buy the real thing. Keep the flow smooth and keep it simple to avoid any confusion. Use only the two main characters or the gist of the story.

Describe what happens in chapter 10 of your book.

_____

_____

_____

_____

_____

_____

_____

_____

_____

_____

_____

_____

_____

Now reduce it to 10 complete simple sentences.

_____

_____

_____

_____

_____

_____

_____

_____

_____

_____

Now reduce it to 5-7 complete complex sentences.

_____

_____

_____

_____

_____

Read aloud and reduce to 3-5 sentences.

_____

_____

_____

_____

Repeat this process for all your other chapters.

Author Bio: Construct a light but serious description about yourself designed to connect to the reader. Tell them about your hobbies or interests, family and so on. Talk about your travels, schooling, or the goals you want to achieve. Or how much fun you had writing this book! Do not ever give away details. Everything you have accomplished can be explained in generalities. Keep it general, yet informative, and above all, relatable.

Spill your guts. Don't hold back. Give it everything you have. Every accomplishment, all your favorite foods, drinks, activities, colors, books. Give it all your history, where you have lived, where you have worked, all of your awards, all of your publications, all of your life. Write a history of you from birth until death - or what you want your life to look like between now and death. I want it all, every dirty detail, every cobweb, every dust ball. Don't forget your pets, every single one of them. Even the frog you snuck into the house to let loose in chemistry class.

113

- Put a single line through everything you don't want your partner to ever find out about.
- Now put a single line through everything you don't want your kids to know about.
- Now put a single line through things you really do not care about any more.
- Now put a single line through the things you don't want a total stranger knowing.

Rewrite what you have left.

_____

_____

_____

_____

_____

_____

_____

_____

_____

_____

_____

_____

_____

_____

_____

_____

_____

_____

_____

_____

_____

_____

_____

Reduce the entire paragraph to 7 - 10 simple sentences. (Long Bio)

_____

_____

_____

_____

_____

_____

_____

_____

_____

Reduce the entire paragraph to 3-5 complex sentences. (Short Bio)

_____

_____

_____

_____

Now you have your personal bio. Now repeat this exercise for your professional bio. Write your final 3-5 complex sentences here.

_____

_____

_____

_____

- **Cover of the book**: You should have the cover of the book as an electronic copy of the front cover of the book. It should be in 72dpi .jpeg format. This is easy enough to transfer through e-mail and clear enough for them to reproduce for their promotional material. You should also have a 300 dpi, .tiff format for actual printing on brochures, bookmarks, postcards, and any other hard printing you need to do.

- **Picture of the Author**: The reader needs to see a high quality, professional, recognizable image of you. Don't do dramatic or fluffy with a lot of glamorous attire. Keep it balanced, down to earth, and practical, with a simple background. You want someone who is looking for you, to recognize you at a book signing. When my son needed senior pictures, I just bought the copyright to them and then I could reproduce as many or as few as I wanted forever. I didn't get a lot of actual pictures, but I also didn't have to order a bunch of pictures I didn't need either.

> **True story**: An author was so excited about their first book they went to a modeling studio to have their picture done for the back of their book and for their publicity packages. A reader attending a book signing walked right up to the author and asked, "Where is this author sitting, please?" showing them their own modeling picture on the back of their own book. It was embarrassing for the author and the reader, that the picture did not look like the author at all! So please be careful with your pictures, and have them done professionally, without much primping if you can afford it. When getting your picture taken, make sure you have all the rights to reproduce that picture as many times as you want. With the digital age this is something you need to make sure to speak to the photographer about, and obtain a written release.

- **Book Description**: You have less than ten words to hook the prospective reader. Another ten words to make them interested, and a final ten words to part them from their dollar. A well written description can, in thirty words or less capture the reader, pull them into a book and make them your biggest fan and your best advertisement. This is what appears on the back of your book, your web site, your publicity package, your posters, your postcards - it is all about your book.

Tell me all about your book. Don't leave out a detail, a twist, a scene, a description. I want to know it all.

_____

_____

_____

_____

_____

_____

_____

_____

_____

- Draw a single line through anything that gives the conclusion away.
- Draw a single line through anything that gives away the major plot points.
- Draw a single line through any details or descriptions.
- Draw a single line through any thing that stands out as specific to this story.

Rewrite what you have left.

_____

_____

_____

_____

_____

_____

_____

_____

_____

120 _____

_____

_____

_____

Rewrite reducing to 7-10 simple sentences. (Long Description)

_____

_____

_____

_____

_____

_____

_____

_____

_____

Rewrite to 3-5 complex sentences. (Short description)

_____

_____

_____

_____

_____

You will require several book summaries. One for the book itself, one for the genre, one each for the sub-genres and then one or two for your expert markets, such as quilting, gardening, religion, hobbies etc.. Research your market for what the market needs in a book description to hook the reader. Read the advertisements for your competition. Look at their book descriptions and pick and choose what they are using to sell their books. If you have read the book, you will most likely find that what they are using to sell their books has very little of the overall story. What it does do is give you what the marketing research has found to be the catch phrase for the market.

After you have researched your book description, look at which markets everyone else is using. Keep it simple and use those markets, too. Now, how many others can you expand into? You will find you need several book descriptions to address different markets your book fits. That is great! **121** Your goal is to grab as many markets as you can. By spreading yourself out, you introduce yourself to many types of readers who talk to their friends.

- **Pitch Sheet**: – This is a standardized format for the buyer.

The sheet includes:

A copy of the Cover
The tag line for book or series
ISBN
Price
Page count
Distributor Discount (This is anywhere between 55% and 60%)
Genre
Language
Book Type
Online and distributor availability

- **Author Page**: This is where you put your wonderful picture, and your long bio together. This is your put together, unstoppable presentation of the author. It should reflect professionalism, a social personality, confidence and success.
- **About the Book**: This also contains 2 main elements. The first is a full color cover of your book. It allows the buyers to decide on its attractiveness and marketability points and allows your reader to find it on the shelf or on the computer. The second is your long book description.
- **Book Reviews:** These are independent opinions of your book. Should the ones you use in your package be positive? Of course! On the other hand they should have a little bit of critique. Although you wrote the best book in the world, you are not going to agree with everyone else's opinion. Make sure the reviews that you use for publicity purposes are balanced. When the individual picks up the book or the sample chapter, you want them to have faith in your reviews to use it for their marketing purposes. It is their reputation that is on the line, just like yours, for anything that isn't honest and truthful.
- **Upcoming Books**: An author who has a writing career is more likely to have support from the buyers and readers. If they really like the first book they are going to want more, more, more. When defining your upcoming books, you should come up with at least three more books to be released in six to nine month intervals. Even if the books are pretty much done – don't push it. Flooding the market can hurt you, too. Pace yourself, and be more concerned about creating a great book. If you have one specific book – such as this one – that you are promoting then push back the release date and work on your pre-press publicity really hard. Concentrate on pre-orders and getting your reputation out there as an expert.

- **Author's Writing Resume**: The more you have the better it is. Make sure this includes everything. If you have written a curriculum, lyrics used in church, or school, a column for a local newsletter, a technical manual you created for your company, these should all be included in your writing resume. Letters to the editor do not count.
- **Summary of Workshops**: Where is your expertise? When looking at fiction books, notice the vast differences in subject matter. We have mystery books, centered around blood hounds that rescue, mysteries that include recipes that are featured in the book, old British traditions and policies of societal structure, and the mysteries that are centered around the everyday aspects of neighborhood or culture. Now is the time to define your expertise. This does not mean you went to school for it or that you have specific training. What it does mean is that you know more about it than the average person. If you garden, belong to a garden club, and know that a hydrangea changes its blooming color by the addition of iron sulfate in the soil, then you can talk about how your experiences with your gardening effects the way you write. The only reason I know this is there is a book where the detective knew this, and looked at the hydrangea in the yard and found the murder weapon – a gun – buried beneath the plant. I actually went to a web site and did some research, it was correct.
- **Author Tour Schedule**: Here is where the fun begins! After you have planned it then market it. The more the book buyers see you doing the more apt they are to support your book signing. Now the double edge sword is that this is the package you are using to try to get book signings. So make a list of places you want to go over the next twelve to eighteen months and put them in here. Although you may not have actual locations yet, that you have a plan is impressive and most people in those positions want to make it work for you.

- **Order Form For Book**: Nobody can pre-order your book if you don't make it available. A full sheet format is easy to follow and allows them to order and pay for the book, yet send it as a gift to someone else. Include ordering information and a place for them to write a personalization as a gift. Order forms for workshops or to request more information should be included. When sending out your press packages, have a reservation form for the workshops. If they know you are willing to travel there is a chance to get paid to do it. They can't offer if they don't know.

- **Author's Web Site**: Eighty-five percent of all books are sold through a web site. Amazon® is the leader in all books sales. Creating a web presence allows your reader and the buyers to instantly connect to you. A foundational duplicate of your press package, creates your web site and fulfills your buyer's need for instant gratification in our society. Although this isn't included in the package, your web site address should be on every page, as well as your e-mail address.

Have all the information in hard copy and in PDF format for distribution. Remember this is about presentation. Here is where your money can be well invested. Your hard copy prints should be in four color copy and placed in either a custom printed folder or a high end presentation folder. The folder should include a disk with the press package in its entirety in PDF format and the copy in .txt format. This makes it easy for the book store to print and distribute what they need for their marketing and have .txt format to create their own flyers and marketing material for their clientele.

Remember making it easy for them to help you means that you can have better support for your book signing. Print up a few to have on hand. Most buyers are going to want this via electronic copy, reducing your costs for printing. Make sure it is perfect.

Chapter Six: Promotional Materials
(Money)

This chapter is an overview of your promotional materials and their uses. There are other mentions of their usage throughout the book, and then as you start using them, you will also find other ways to use them. Remember that marketing is a brave marriage of common sense and imagination. Put yourself out there; turn every "no" into a "maybe" and then into a "yes". Be kind, generous, helpful, positive and confident. If you do, you will find yourself going further than anyone, including yourself, thought you would.

Of course, with all of your grand marketing intentions, never forget to keep an eye on your budget. This chapter will outline your greatest money sinks, which are mainly in the production of the marketing materials. You need to have these items produced in a professional manner. If you run a graphic design studio, or do a lot of photography and have the high end programs and printers necessary, then your costs will be slightly lower. You may wish to print your material on your little home photo printer, but that is expensive, and hiring a professional printer gives you better quality. True, it is more expensive up front, but cheaper per unit. You want the professional status, so use the professional services.

Accepted rules governing Galley copies

There are industry standard rules for the manipulation and use of galleys or Advanced Reading Copies (ARC). Professionals that you will be contacting should adhere to these rules knowing that by not doing so they are cutting into your profit. The ISBN (International Standard Book Number) is removed from the back cover so that an individual cannot take the book to a book store and return it for profit. Without the ISBN barcode the book is not traceable and cannot be returned to a distributor for a refund. When you are giving your books to reviewers, endorsers, buyers, or readers, the lack of the ISBN on the back cover denotes you as a professional in the eyes of other professionals.

ARCs should not be sold for profit. As you are giving them away it is not an accepted practice for them to be resold. The drawback is that individuals have started collecting them, creating an online market for them as collectibles and a market for them in the used book stores. So galleys should only go to respected professionals in the business. Keep track of them so you can run interference if they show up on line. Accept that if you give an ARC to a private individual they will sell it for profit on line or at a used book store. For this reason many small publishers do not use ARCs any longer. It is a risk, but definitely distinguishes you as a professional and not some over night wannabe author.

The biggest difference between these and your final published book is the lack of an (ISBN) on the back cover. That area is replaced with your projected marketing information. Verbiage denoting it as a promotional copy is placed in full view on the front and the back covers.

ARC's are necessary, useful and one of the most formidable marketing tools available to you. In a snapshot this gives the person you are handing it to the image of exactly the product they are buying and a glimpse of what you have in mind for the future. They know almost instantly if you are going to make them money or not. This is publicity, a calling card in this industry and should never be cut from the budget.

Promotional Packages

Think of a promotional package as a portfolio of your work. A promotional package showcases your work, markets your high points and allows a catalog type presentation of all your offerings. You have already completed an entire chapter in this book just on the promotional package and what it should contain. There are also several places that explain how to use it effectively. So why do we mention it here? Because it is that IMPORTANT!

Think of going to an art show and looking at the paintings on the walls. There is a catalog available for those interested in purchasing an item. This catalog details the birth of each piece, the history behind each piece, the summary of the meaning of each piece and the overall expectation of the piece. Your promotional package does the same thing for you. It shows your workshops, your creative work, your professional work and your journey all in one single place. This is what industry professionals are going to judge your professional persona on.

126

Postcards

Postcards are great to have for promotional purposes. Hand them out to strangers on the street before your book comes out, leave them laying around the hotels you visit, the doctor's office, anyplace where someone can pick it up and follow through. We use 4" by 6" post card size because they are small enough to slip into a purse or pocket, but not small enough to get lost among the other slips or paper or business cards that accumulate through the normal day.

Postcards are also used to announce a book signing. The front stays the same but the back of the card has information on an upcoming book signing at a particular location. You prep about 500 and send them about 4-6 weeks before the event. The bookstores put them in the bags of customers or leave them lying out.

Business Cards

Business or calling cards are something everyone uses. They slide them politely in their wallet, pocket, purse, or briefcase, only to lose them in a Rolodex® system, their electronic files, or the nearest waste can. To keep your business card in the hands of the industry professionals you want to stay in contact with, make your card something useful they want to hang on to.

The back of my business cards contain five simple hints for hiring an editor, or five publicity hints that writers will use for a long time. So how do you do it? Define what your passion is, figure out how you live it and come up with three to five reminders of how others can do it. Put those on the back of your card and you will find that people not only hang on to your card, but they talk about it.

Publicity Posters

Publicity posters need to be sent to places you will be appearing. Posters should include the following basic information: The short summary of your book. Your Book Cover. Your Professional Picture. Arrange the items on your poster in a way that you can change the times and dates of your appearances. Velcro attached colored foam board is handy and reusable, for attaching changing dates and times.

If you are actively marketing, you will need about ten posters. Mail them out to stores (or appearance sites) about four weeks before your appearance and pick them up after your appearance. Then take off the appearance information, replace it with the next one, and mail them away again.

There are two standard sizes, 36" by 24" and 18" by 24". The larger size is generally preferred as it can be hung nicely in a window or placed on an easel. Having a smaller size, 11" by 14" to sit by your table or on your product table at the rear of the room is a nice touch. The more the audience is reminded that you are an expert, the more sales you are likely to achieve.

Thank You Card

The idea of personalized and hand written thank you cards for a show of appreciation are quickly becoming a thing of the past. It doesn't matter how electronically adept you are, a simple hand written thank you card goes a long way to showing your appreciation for someone's efforts. Yes I understand that they received something out of the deal, and that they were only doing their job, but isn't any effort that benefits you and your goals worth ten minutes of your time? The cards do make an impression, will get you remembered and you are more likely to be invited back.

Kindness and consideration are two of the most powerful tools you have as an author. Most of the people you are going to be dealing with on a professional level have to deal with people who are rude, discourteous, bossy and all around just disgruntled. Your smile, kindness, and consideration can erase the negativity of ten people and make you memorable in a positive light to the professional you are trying to work with. Just taking a short breath after they have snapped your head off, to acknowledge their frustration, will get you more reasons to say thank you to them, than if you didn't.

Kindness and consideration are two of the most powerful tools you have as an author.

Chapter Seven: Author Web Site
(Time and Money)

Eighty-five percent of all books are sold through the internet. This number is increasing as electronic books for the book readers increase. Electronic sales, publishing and advertising are on the rise. It is low cost, the security is great and the Congressional laws being passed to protect its users are actually working. The drawback to everyone's addiction to the internet is that if you don't have a web site, and an Amazon Author page, and a Fantastic Fiction page and a few articles, and, and, and, and … OR an electronic presence, you won't get anything from the public. When hearing about a new author or book, the first thing that buyers do is go to the internet and look them up. Even as little as five to seven years ago, having an author web site was considered an extra expense, now it is mandatory. Without a web site no one will know who you are, show up for a book signing, book an appearance or buy your book. A web site gives you legitimacy, credibility and professional status. The good news about creating a web site is that the majority of the copy for your web site will be completed when you finish your publicity package. Everything that is in your publicity package goes into your web site, each item as a separate tab or menu option.

Without a web site, no one will know who you are.

You can choose either to have the web site designed by a professional or purchase one from any number of companies on the internet. The ones that can be purchased are significantly less; however, depending on your goals, may not be right for what you need. Using these sites will also take a lot of your time and effort unless you are truly internet savvy or have a friend who can help you. If you use a professional, make sure they have been recommended by people you know, and check them out yourself. Either way, setting up the page will be very important to your overall plan.

Of course, the web site should have several added items not found in a publicity package. Let's start with the nearest and dearest to our heart, the e-commerce page for allowing people to buy your books. How you set this up is dependent on how much profit you want to make versus how much time you want to invest. Easier but less profitable, link your book's buy page to a trusted on-line site such as Amazon®.com or BN.com. When you are selling thousands of books this is a good alternative, even if the retailers do take up to sixty percent of your cover price to cover their expenses and time. Remember this is a business, and they have to make money too. The harder and most profitable way is to fill the orders yourself and ship them daily. Here are some guidelines and helpful hints for doing that.

First, remember that this falls into your time investment budget. You always have to have books on hand. If you have the option of having the buyer request you to personalize the book either for the buyer or for a friend, you have to do that also. You have twenty-four hours from the moment that you process that payment to ship the book. Even pre order payments cannot be processed until the book ships.

Use pick up service either with one of the overnight services, (you might need to do a little research to see who is the cheapest in your area), and have them packaged and shipped with 2-3 day shipping. You don't want someone who has paid for the book to wait ten days to get it via media mail. They will lose their enthusiasm for your book. Also, sending it media mail does not give you a way to track it. If you cannot track the book and it is lost, then you are out a bunch of money. First you have to refund the money they paid for the book, and then you are charged a fee for the refund. So it is in your best interest to use the tracking numbers provided by the shipping agencies. All of these shipping agencies allow for online ordering, pickup and shipping. So figure out which one works best for you in your area and use it.

Contents of your Web Site

Beyond your promotional package, here is a list of things that should be added to your web site.

• **Keep** your audience coming back with a blog and an electronic newsletter. Pick a theme for your newsletter and then stick with it. If you are writing fiction it can be a monthly family letter from your characters, catching people up like most do at the end of the year. If you are already running a blog that does this then pick another theme, maybe one related to your book, such as cooking, gardening, quilting, pottery, or outdoor stuffs. Keeping the reader engaged between releases is important for the release of the next book.

• **Congressional** law states that you have to use the double opt-in process to avoid being listed and prosecuted as spam. This is something you have done to acquire a social networking account as well as any other numerous accounts. The first is they sign in on your page – opt-in number one. The second is the activation of the account through e-mail notification - opt-in number two. As soon as this is done, you will send your newsletter to just a single e-mail and it will go to everyone on your list.

• **Don't** ask your customers for a ton of information! If you do, they probably won't sign up. Remember, they probably have very little time and they have already heard lots of horror stories about criminals who scam them, hack into their computer, or steal their identity. Keep it simple and they will come back for more! Once they get to know you they can add whatever information they feel comfortable with as your relationship grows. The more novels they purchase, the more they learn about your characters and you.

85% of all books are sold through the internet.

- **Post** a short story or sneak peak of the upcoming chapters on your web site. Short stories are better than giving away your next book. This would fall into the double opt-in structure as well as the newsletter. A short story is defined by ten chapters or less, totaling around 150 pages. Make sure it is written in its totality and then professionally edited. You need to take as much care with this writing as you did with your novel. If you make a silly mistake, the reader will catch it and may not purchase your next book. Post a chapter a week and send notice through the double opt-in letter that a new chapter has been posted. After you have completed posting the story, ask for input as to what your readers would want to see in the next installment. An added benefit to a short story posting, is now you have an outline for a full size novel if you want, an in between short story that allows the story to move forward without creating a full novel.

Keep it exciting and current.

- **Include** your favorite web site pages. This is a good way for readers with similar interests to find you. Limit the amount of favorite links to ten, any more than ten becomes too cumbersome to keep track of. Broken links are annoying and prospective readers may think you do not care enough for your site to upkeep it. If you don't care enough about your site then do you really care enough about your books? To make sure your links are accurate and up to date, check your site monthly from public machines, this means a machine you do not use on a regular basis. Just go to your public library, go to your web page and click on the links on your favorite page. Fix any broken links as soon as possible. Also have a way on your web pages for anyone to report broken links.

- **Finally**, have your standard information pages. Have your social networking links, your blog link, Amazon author page link, Twitter®, etc. These can all be individual links or on a single page. The more working links you have, the higher you fall in the search engines and the greater your chance of being known.

- **Remember** that your web page cannot become boring or stagnant. With more of your time focused on running around the country being famous, accepting accolades and awards, or just stuck in some cabin writing, you cannot forget your web pages. There should be new information on them at least once a week. You can do this yourself or through any number of programs or hire someone to do it. If you allow your web pages to grow stagnant then the readers are going to think that you aren't writing anymore and they will stop looking for your next installment. Just add it to the weekly task list.

Chapter Eight: Building Your Author Persona
(Time, lots and lots of time)

Your author persona is one of the most important attributes of your new career. This is you reputation. This is how people see you, how they judge you and where you stand in their buying experience. There is a standard to be upheld, and for each individual reader, standard changes based on the preference and what they are reading. Your goal is to be the standard that everyone else is held up to. Go back to your competition lists and research. Look at the standard of the author that you wish to be, and make that the minimum you are willing to settle for, and grow from there. Remember that it is a perception. Your perception is not going to be the same as anyone else, because you are not them. Therefore, the only person you are accountable to is you; when you think you are there, then push it higher, never settle and always move for the next level of excellence. With time, effort and winning those epic battles, you will achieve your success as you see it. My success with this book will be authors that travel more, talk more, interact more, and work together more to create a new level of literary excellence for the readers in the world like me.

Be Patient!

Articles

Writing articles is an easy way to promote your expertise, put your name out there as a professional, hit higher on the internet search engines and in general validate you as a professional to the publishing industry. There are several other benefits to writing articles. You may get paid. People may wish you to speak to their groups or conventions based on your expertise. Since you need to do appearances and interviews anyway, getting invited, all expense paid travel, to conferences is a great way to supplement your tour budget.

There are three main venues for article publication: specific web sites where you are a featured contributor, article databases which act as a clearing house for all subject matters, and hard copy printing such as magazines, literary journals, or newspaper. Each of these has its own hurdles and can be time consuming.

Where do you find these places? Start with periodicals and web sites that you currently read. Your voice will be similar to those that you read, so it will be easier to break into those realms. Then spread out and search and research other venues. I wish I could sit here and give you a fool proof plan to make it all happen, but it takes research and time to find what suits you best, and what will give you the best, more legitimate and complete exposure. **The most important piece of advice is to be patient.**

Established periodic publishing companies have a peer review system in place, but peer review does not happen overnight. Do not be surprised or impatient if it takes weeks to get your article posted. Use response time as part of your criteria for choosing where you post. You need a review system, just not one that takes an eon to happen.

The frequency and quality of publishing is the most important portion of this process. People who follow you will be looking for your new articles every week. For maximum effectiveness you should be submitting five, but no less than three, different articles per week to five different online publications. For print publications you should be researching and submitting no less than one a week and no more than three per week. Any more than this will make it too cumbersome to do your follow up and tracking.

Online articles should not exceed two hundred fifty words per article. Your articles should be micro targeted and specific. For example, you shouldn't write about plot or character development. These topics are too general and overdone. Your article will get lost in the crowd. Instead, narrow your topic to creating support for your plot or character habits. Write about developing different aspects of your plot, or how to use a word and it's many faceted meanings or any number of specific items related just to your interests and expertise. Using this chapter as an example, there are several articles that can be written from this base: "Peer Review", "Defining Article Subjects", Using the Article Database", "Reading a Masthead", "Submission Etiquette", "Styles of Writing for the Internet", and the list goes on and on.

With hard copy articles you need to follow the submission guidelines of the periodical you are writing for. These submission guidelines, upcoming themes and person to submit to are usually published on the periodicals' web site. Again, go for the comfort zone. If you read it, you can write for it. Submit all articles at least six months before the publication date. Christmas articles are usually submitted by June or July. Hard copy magazines have completed their production period about three to four months before they are released to print.

This is your expert status. If you are writing about writing, then you are an expert in writing. Your online articles will be about how you employ your techniques with your hard copy print and books examples of your techniques. If your articles are about gardening, quilting, etc, then your articles will show your hints and tips, while your short stories and books will incorporate the passion that you feel for what you do. Everything is intertwined and works together to make your professional presence more legitimate and well received.

Contests

Contests are another form of peer review. Just a simple search of Literary Contests for 2011 netted over 11.6 million hits on Google® on August 26, 2011. Some of them are good and some of them are less than stellar. Some of the less stellar ones are the ones that hit in the top of the list because they know how to use the web for marketing. Contests have restrictions that range from word count to ethnicity of the author. Researching contests may be one of your greatest electronic time sinks. There are some you just want to be considered for, such as *The National Book Awards*. Knowing that the competition is stiff and the qualifications are not easy to meet, everyone who qualifies should at least enter, every time they can.

Contests have stricter submission guidelines than any other venue. If you don't meet those guidelines, you are out AND they get to keep your money. Those are the rules. The guidelines for what are considered legitimate literary contests are fluctuating with the times and the changes in the industry. Make sure to look at your writer's support sites to check the validity of any contest before you enter.

A lot of publishing companies, smaller ones, tend to run a contest to find works that they want to publish, and will offer a publishing contract as the grand prize. Getting your book to a publisher and printed is the easy part of this race. You can do it yourself or use any of the subsidy presses that are out there. A publicity support package is the key to success, not just a book in print. Now a publishing contract with a marketing package and marketing support that is a real win! For the sake of respectability and legitimacy, there should be a monetary prize for your efforts.

All of the prizes aside, the highest benefit you get from entering a contest is the chance to put "Award Winning Author" on everything you use for publicity. Award Winning pushes you up a few notches in the realm of the readers and the buyers. Even if it just an "Honorary Mention", it means that you went through the review process and came out with positive feedback about your work.

Check the guidelines again! Make sure you are following them. Make sure your submission package is complete. Check the deadline and make sure you make it. Send your submission with delivery confirmation. Do not try to call and find out if they have it, they have thousands, so just make sure it was delivered. Follow any deadlines and postings on their web site or e-mail as to where your book is in the phase of judging. As an entrant you are entitled to a full release of the placement of the books when the contest is over. Make sure you get that and any other information about your title in particular that they are willing to share. **135**

Even if you win nothing or it takes years to get one of your articles in hard copy form, remember that it is the fact that you are going through the process that makes you legitimate and respectable, not the winning status. These types of peer reviews can be equated to having a review of your job performance. Even the big guys didn't get perfect reviews or their articles published the first time. An author who is anyone, started just where you are right now. They made it and so can you!

Endorsements & Critiques

Getting peer reviews and critiques separate the professionals from the vanity writers. If you want to be a professional writer, you need them. Entering the peer review and critique arena is not for the light hearted or easily offended. The entire process is not for a pat on the back or to tell you how good you are; it is for an honest and highly opinionated review of the high and low points of your story, your presentation, your grammar, your style and overall beliefs that are reflected in your characters. Peer review and critique individuals do not care if they hurt your feelings. They are there for the benefit of the market and consumers who look to them for guidance.

Endorsements

An endorsement is one or two lines, usually less than fifteen words that support your book. You see them on the backs of books, generally from well known authors of the same genre or if the book is non-fiction, from an established organization such as the *Heart Association* or *The Art Glass Association*, validating the publications' usefulness and correctness.

To procure endorsements, the first thing you need is an endorsement package. This package is simple to produce and submit. Start with the short synopsis and bio from your press package, add the chapter by chapter synopsis and then a galley copy of the book. Submit it with a cover letter to the organization or person who has agreed to review the material. Make sure to thank them for their time and consideration.

All e-mail programs have an option to turn on a read receipt and delivery receipt. This is an excellent way to keep track of who has received what and when.

You also need to include an endorsement page. This can have several unique choices, no more than five, that the endorser can choose from, and also includes a space where they can write their own. Make sure you include a self addressed stamped envelope for them to return the form, or remind them of the process that you discussed when they agreed to review your work for endorsement.

So how do you get them to review your work for an endorsement? This is where your networking and socializing becomes one of the most important things you have ever done. Attending conventions and writing workshops, keeping up your social networking pages and blogs, and reaching out and touching those that inspire you, are the way you get endorsements. The people you ask for endorsements should already be published in your genre, or for the non-fiction crowd be a recognized professional in the subject and industry you are writing for.

If you haven't attended any conventions or seminars and collected those valuable contacts, then your next best bet is the social networking sites. Almost every large named author has a presence through one of these sites. They gain notoriety with the number of friends that they have. Just like all relationships you have to be considerate, take time to learn who the professional is as a person rather than a celebrity and then ask for their advice on how to go through this process. It is forward and rude to come right out and ask them to do it. Be friendly and get to know them and you will find they are more inclined to help you.

Visiting and connecting through professional web sites is another way to network and collect guidance in attaining endorsements. As you become a regular, you can quietly and privately ask for a little guidance and most people are willing to help. Even the big authors review most of their own e-mails, or at least have the interesting ones brought to their attention. Just remember to be considerate, kind, and respectful. If you are contacting them, so are a million others. Remember honey attracts more bees than vinegar.

Endorsement Etiquette

Do not think for one micro second that the person you are requesting the endorsement from is actually going to read your book. They will most likely have a member of their staff review the package you sent and look at your promotional material to gauge if their endorsement is going to net them anything at all. Remember that this is a business. If they endorse your book, they are going to expect to get a minimal return on their time, and it is minimal at best. That is why you submit the chapter by chapter, short synopsis and bio. Most of the endorsements come strictly from those three items.

Then why send the book? That is just a little extra protection for you. The following story has never been validated, but it stops and makes you think:

A major non-fiction author who has sold millions of books was asked to endorse a book based on the three items that are standard for submission. He was never sent the book itself. When the book was released and hit the market, the endorser's fan base was appalled that he supported a book that went directly against his professional and moral code. When the endorser found out he asked to have his endorsement removed and the author refused. Litigation was involved and the author found that he had to remove the book with the endorsement from the shelves; based on false representation. This cost the author a great deal of money from the legal costs, to the reprinting of the thousands of books with new covers, without the endorsement. There is no way to track the loss of sales due to the removal of the endorsement, or the damage to his reputation. If the author had submitted the book along with the package there would have been no room for misrepresentation on the author's part and the author's reputation would have stayed intact.

After the process is completed, and even if you do not get an endorsement, a hand written thank you card for their time and effort is required. They may not do it the first time, but at least that leaves an avenue open for you to approach them again with a different project. In this business, you never burn a bridge that cannot be rebuilt. It is all about your reputation and how the public perceives it.

List 5 things about your book that make it endorsable:

_____

_____

_____

_____

_____

Support endorsement 3 with 3 ideas.

Reduce to 15 words or less

---

138 Reduce to 10 words or less

Reduce to 5 words or less

Now apply this exercise to your other 4 ideas.

The final five word endorsements are what is included in your endorsement package. Make sure you come up with at least fifteen unique, and stand alone endorsements so that endorsers are not picking the same one. When one is used, remove if from the choices and make another one. You can have too many endorsements from a single market. So go back to your lists in the beginning of this book and list as many different markets as you can, and try to get an endorsement from each market.

Critiques

Critiques are one of the toughest things to take. Asking for a critique shows that you are strong and confident enough to ask for a professional opinion of the one thing that is almost as close to your heart as your first born. A critique will have parts in it that are hard for you to read. It will discuss parts of your work as if they weren't your perfect child. Remember, it is a single person's opinion! It is not a general consensus, it is not a personal attack, and it is not the ultimate authority. It is one person's reflection. This reflection could be affected by the day they are having, for good or bad. Try to understand. Writing is your work, but it is based on your mood. Do not be hard on them. You asked for it. Know that you are going to feel like you were kicked in the teeth. Critiques are not for the faint of heart, but it is a necessary evil to being a professional in the literary business.

By the way, having friends and family review or critique does NOT count! Most of the time they will not tell you the truth. Oh, they will say they're telling you the truth, but when you really start asking in depth questions, you will find that they have more to tell you than you originally thought. You are going to need other writers, people in your writing group, critique group and/or professionals to tell you the truth. Having a thick skin and open mind is necessary. Sometimes you won't like what they have to say. Let me rephrase that: Most of the time you won't like what they have to say. But you are serious, right? You really want to do this, right? Then what are you waiting for? This is just the beginning of one part of the wonderful writing career you want!

Literary critiques are an entirely different animal, and the term animal is the nicest term we can use. Wild demon from the fiery pits of the bowels of a volcano would be far more accurate. *Dictionary. com* defines critique as "to analyze critically." Literary Critiques are an unbiased judgment of your work completed by someone not aligned with you or any group you are with; think restaurant critic. When searching for groups that provide critiques of your work, it is preferred that it be an unpaid critique, with the general consensus being that if you paid for it than it will slant in your favor and cannot be unbiased. There are several companies that will provide you with critiques that you pay for and that the industry accepts as valid and applicable. So do your research and make sure that you aren't wasting your money. First, use the internet to search for places that provide literary critiques on a submission basis. You will find that most literary critiques are completed by educational facilities, but some are done by critiquing agents. The name of the game is research.

You asked for it.

Critiquing agents are genre specific, so research the top ten for your genre. It may be fairly easy to find those genres that could be considered more academic, young adult, poetry, biographies, non-fiction or what classifies as the great American Novel. There are critiquing agents out there for pop fiction and general fiction. You just need to look for them.

Remember that each critiquing agent, just like reviewers and readers in this industry, receive thousands of requests for critiquing. They use their submission guidelines filter. Check their submission guidelines the day you mail, and make sure all of your publicity propaganda is complete so assembling a package should be a breeze. Make sure your cover letter is personalized.

The process takes time, so this is normally done before the book is available to the public. Even if your book is currently available it isn't too late. Your chances of a critique are lower, but not impossible. Go through the motions and see what you can come up with. As with everything else, a hand written thank you note is your final step.

CHAPTER NINE: CREATING A TOUR SCHEDULE
(Time and Fun)

I love my editing job. It is great because I get to read all the time, but that is not the best part. The best part comes from the my author's first book signing. I attend every one that I can. There I sit in the back of the room and watch the author, and usually, I am standing next to their hardest critic. I watch as the critic moves from ambiguity to proud as the people approach the author and talk to them about their creation. That is the best part of my job. That first book signing and the awareness and awe of completion for everyone involved.

There are a few things to remember in creating your tour schedule. The first is that you are only going to be busy for a few hours a day. So you will have a lot of time on your hands in between. So the first step is to find someplace you want to go. Put down how much time you want to travel and the best times to travel to the areas you want to go. Make sure there are sights and sounds that interest you in your location. The second is moderation; if you over schedule and start lagging at the end, then your performance will be less than stellar, and affect the overall relationship with your host. So moderation in scheduling is a key. The third and final thing to remember is that you

The only person you are accountable to is you.

are there to enjoy yourself, so make sure that whatever you choose to do is not all a task. There are certain aspects of everything that you do that you are going to like more than others; but try to make sure that seventy percent of the stuff that you do is fun, twenty percent is just mediocre and ten percent is "I can't stand this stuff." You will then have a successful schedule that results in wonderful professional relationships and something taken off of the Bucket List. You will return to your daily grind feeling positive, refreshed and productive.

When creating a travel schedule you are going to want to create it several months in advance. You are not going to want to set it all up at one time, but you should at least have an idea for the year where you want to go. This can be as extreme as, "I have a month of vacation and I want to take it all at one time," to, "I have a weekend a month and I can only drive four hours each way." Everyone has their limitations: finances, time, or maybe traveling is just part of that 10% of the job that you just plain don't want to do. Be aware and embrace those limitations; do not try to overcome them or force them into something they are not. Work within them and you will find that they are really not limitations at all, but more like guidelines to keep you comfortable and happy.

Creating a schedule

Make a list of friends or relatives who want to see you and you haven't made the time for. Plan a visit and work a little on the side. They will be accommodating and understanding, and more than likely you will find your friends and family standing in the back cheering you on. Then it is on to the celebration party and reconnecting with your friends and family.

Make a list of things you want to see. Try small to begin with; getting a book signing in New York is not an easy feat. Remember that this is a list, not a contract, so nothing you put down on paper is mandatory, just ideas, dreams and hopes that can slowly be fulfilled. Using your recognized limitations you are embracing, prioritize the list and decide how you want to move forward.

Do you have another passion such as quilting or pottery? Do you already travel with someone who does festivals, shows or anything of that ilk? Then take that schedule and make arrangements around them. If this is something that you have been doing with them for a period of time, you already know the people to contact to start the ball rolling. That schedule is set pretty far in advance, so you have the lead time you need.

Do you not really want to travel outside of your area? Most of us live within an hour or two of a major metropolis. Having access not only to that big city but also to the outlying bedroom communities and small towns that make up the metropolitan area and everything in between. You can do numerous events in the smaller towns as well as in the big city, without ever leaving your back yard.

Scheduling time

Most organizations or businesses want at least six months notice. Some are putting together their calendars almost two years out, some only sixty days out. Calling and asking for something to happen next week, is going to be a waste of time for you and them. No one has enough time to do any advertising and individuals who want to attend most likely have plans set that they can't reschedule. Have this plan last for eighteen months or more. You can take breaks in between, but make sure you have dates filled.

Start with finding out when and how their appearance schedules are booked. Then rearrange and tweak your schedule to match theirs. You need them to want you, so do everything you can so they do not have to exert any effort to have you. If they have very little effort or time involved, then you are more likely to get that booking.

No Excuses

Now, "**I have a full time job and can't do that.**" That is not true. You have some evenings, your weekends, your vacation time and your holidays. All it takes is a little planning. Make your tour exciting. Go places that you want to see and visit. You only have to be present for book signing for about two hours. Include one hour before and one hour after and then you are done. What do you do with the rest of the weekend? Hike the Grand Canyon, go white water rafting, kayak the Missouri river, visit the Smithsonian Museum of Art. There are a great deal of hidden treasures in our own backyards, places to not only enrich your life, but to keep you from getting bored. Even if it is a local cave in the middle of nowhere, but only fifteen minutes from where you are doing your signing, it is someplace new you haven't been. You are adventurous enough to write a book, publish it and share it with the world, now think of how that book can lead you to adventures you never had taken before. Besides, it is all research for your next book.

"It is expensive and I can't afford it." Remember that this book is written and presented as if you had all the time in the world and all the money in the world. You can't do any of it without some money, but you are creative, you wrote a book. Try to come up with creative ways that are more time invested rather than money invested. Most of that would be internet marketing, and doing free stuff that gets you free press. So use it.

"I can't afford the hotels." The easy answer to this is stay in a cheap one, but much to my accountant's chagrin even I won't stoop that low. It is a high level business hotel or bust for me. I don't get enough sleep as it is, so put me on one of those cheap beds or rooms that don't get dark and my fun for the traveling is over. So, solutions? There are several writing associations out there, either on a state or national level, that have members with guest rooms that open them up to other members. You have to be established and active in the organization, and most likely be able to reciprocate on some level. It is an inexpensive way to travel with some drawbacks. So make sure you look at all the options available to you.

Staying with friends and family is always a good choice if they have room. There are hostels and shared units, or just be really creative and if the weather permits, camp. Think of all the beautiful things you will see with just a pup tent and an air mattress. Rent a travel trailer and pull it behind you. Just as with everything else you are only limited by your imagination.

143

The end of this chapter is what we call the *"__Do ya really want it? Do ya?__"* speech. If you want this, really want it, to the core of your being, you will find ways to do it and afford it. There is not going to be anything to stop you. Excuses are just another hurdle, another issue. A wall that you are building yourself; mortaring with your lack of commitment to yourself and your dream. This is not an industry where money is the driving power for those that produce the product. If you think it is to make money from your book sales, think again. You do this because you want it, because it consumes you, chases you in your sleep, and drives you to share with the world. If you want it, really want it, then you will make it happen.

No Excuses !

Chapter Ten: Smile And Dial
(Time , time, time and time. Coffee helps.)

Cold calling is the bane of all sales. The entire idea of calling a complete stranger, introducing yourself and making small talk with someone who doesn't really want to talk to you any way, is one of the most intimidating experiences in this business. This is your first impression that you make with a person who has the ability to buy your book and is usually the first contact with a real buyer and your first commercial support person. What happens if you stutter, drop the phone, forget the title of your book? This is a scary and yet necessary part of the book business. Book signings and appearances are necessary to your success in the short and the long run. Remember these relationships you make now will be relationships that you will have for years to come. You should be scared, just a little bit; it makes you better at it.

Relationships you make now will be relationships that you will have for years to come

Cold calls are about attitude, confidence and your friendliness. By calling it a 'Cold Call' you have already set the stage of negativity. I currently live in the Midwest, and I can verify that cold is not comfortable, it is not inviting and it is not nice. Get a little bit of a breeze going and it is down right nasty. So first out of the box is a change in how you approach the dreaded cold call. So if you are calling from the dead of winter in the Midwest - think of a warm California beach first, with your favorite drink and beach chair service.

This change in attitude starts with a change in terminology, "Smile and Dial." Who can say no to a smile. Why wouldn't someone want to share your cheerful attitude and be inspired to have an upbeat attitude if you do. Think of it this way, you see someone who isn't smiling and you share yours. Pretty soon they are smiling and sharing your smile with everyone else they see. For the most part it doesn't matter what type of day they have had, someone's kind smile lifted them. Your smile has infused them with more positive energy, more confidence, more energy. Now take all of that positive and enthusiastic energy and push it through the phone, and you start with a smile - and a well rehearsed script.

Here are some general guidelines to follow for success with your Smile and Dial:

• **The** first is never call on a Monday or a Friday, for anything. On Monday they are trying to get through what was left that they didn't finish on Friday as they were dashing out of the office for as long of a weekend as they can get. Friday they are just trying to get out of the office.

- **Never** call first thing in the morning, last thing in the afternoon, or during the traditional two hours for lunch. Your best hours to call are between ten and noon and two and four in the afternoon. Things tend to slow down during those times and people are looking for something to do.

- **Do** not call more than once a week and allow a full week for a return call. If you are calling more often the person you are trying to reach may feel harried or harassed. You are not the only person they are talking to, or trying to talk to them. Be polite, courteous and give them some room to operate.

- **Never** apologize.

The Guidelines

- **Call** the book store and ask for the person in charge of public events or scheduling events at that location. If that person isn't available, make sure to get a name, and time that they are scheduled to be in the office.

- **When** you reach that person make sure you check their tone. Being aware that if they sound harried, busy or just annoyed will go a long way in dealing with them. Remember that you want them to work for you so you have to be aware of what they are doing.

- **If** they sound harried or busy, offer to call them back at a more convenient time. They will note your kindness and will most likely put aside whatever was distracting them to talk to you, with a better attitude. Here you go. You have less than 10 seconds to tell them your name, what you write, and why you think that their store is the best fit for you. Use your previous worksheets on writing copy to choose what is best to say here. It will change from store to store based on the demographics or area.

- **You** close this ten seconds with a question of what they would like to see on their desk, how they would like it to be delivered, via email or snail mail. Most likely they are going to want it via e-mail so make sure you have everything ready to go. See the section on preparing your press package and make sure you send the correct sized files. Make sure you have the correct spelling of their name and their correct e-mail. Read it back to them just to make sure.

- **You** have less than thirty minutes to get them this information with a wonderful short e-mail thanking them for their time and consideration and that you look forward to hearing from them. From here most of your communication will be via e-mail.

- **One** week later, if you haven't heard from them send an email asking them if they would like any additional information and a good time to contact them to set up a book signing. This is also the e-mail that you let them know that you have posters, postcards, bookmarks, press releases and announcements to go out about the book signing. This will show them that you have a monetary investment as well as time commitment to the success of your book signing.

- **Confirm** the book signing and offer to give a free workshop to any of their groups. If you have a children's book ask to have a reading or if you have an adult book ask to talk to any reading groups they have there as part of what you do. A positive attitude will get you anywhere you need to go.

The Script

Using the guidelines above write your Smile and Dial script.

Hello my name is _____

I am a local/visiting author. My inquiry is to arrange a book signing . The title of the

book is _____; it is a

_____; and was published by   **147**

_____. I would also like to

include a visit with your _____
(insert special interest group such as a children's group, reading group, writing group etc.). What information do you require and what is the next step to make this happen?

(Reply from book store representative.)

What time are you available next week to set up the event?

(Reply from book store representative)

Thank you for your time, I will be sending the information before the end of the work day today. I look forward to speaking with you next week.

Dodges and Ducks

It is very likely that you are going to get some dodges and ducks to avoid actually setting an appearance. Remember that this is normal. A flat out, "We don't do book signings or appearances through this store," does NOT mean you can't get it. They have special interest groups; contact the head of that group. Most of that information is on the web site for the store. You won't be able to sell books there, but you will get talk to people, tell them about your book, and let them know where you will be and when they can purchase it. Remember that the main reason for the appearance is the press releases that get your name out in the public eye so your name and title is seen so often it becomes familiar and you become a known entity. It takes about an average of about fifteen to twenty times within a forty five day period for your name to become familiar.

Be ready with yours or your publishing company's procedure and policies on consignments, ordering times, distribution, return policies and acquisition time. The store representative by nature does not have the time to mess with an appearance, and does not want to add the effort to their plate; they have a lot to do already. So do not be discouraged that they don't think you are as wonderful as you really are. Just remember they are people who are working for a company and not you, therefore, you are not their highest priority.

Chapter Eleven: Supporting Your Book Signing
(Time and Money, mostly Time)

Distribution of marketing material is the number one and most productive way to promote a book signing or appearance. There are several approaches to distributing this marketing propaganda. Your entire goal is to create a familiarity between you and the prospective client. You already have a book signing, at an established bookseller, so the question is how to attract customers who already read and already have a relationship with that store to your event.

Our first and most productive bit of advertising is to create postcards. The front of your postcard has the cover of the book, the back has scheduled book signing: With store location, time of the event and the short synopsis you wrote in the earlier chapters of this book. These postcards are usually placed in the bags of customers before the book signing. You want to have them there at least 1 month before the scheduled book signing for the most exposure. How many post cards is that? It is about five hundred a book signing. It seems like a lot, but a single book sold will pay for fifty of them so it is in your benefit to blanket the world with them.

The second thing that you use to create familiarity is a poster. These posters were described in an earlier chapter. Posters are delivered to the site of the event at least three weeks in advance. Call at two weeks out and make sure

Create a new level of literary excellence for the readers in the world.

they have them out and that there isn't anything else they need. These posters are placed in their major windows, with copies of your book, creating a stir for their customers that want to meet you and spend time learning about your book and why you do what you do.

If you don't have a free workshop through the event location, set one up at the local library. Free events get you tons of coverage at absolutely no cost. This coverage is vast and only limited by the time you have to invest. Starting with the most obvious, your hosting location will be doing advertising for you because it is free and they get funding for these types of workshops. Make sure to give back. If someone is hosting you and you are providing a free workshop - then give back. Most likely it is at a library or community building; give ten percent of your sales back to them. They have done a lot of on your behalf with the marketing and promoting - in addition to what you did. Make sure that your thank you note includes that. Now for your turn.

Panel discussions with one or more authors or professional speakers tend to result in more attendees. So after you have your schedule set, contact other authors or professional speakers in the area and see if you can organize a panel. Other ideas are providing discounts, or refer a friend programs. Look at what other successful marketers are doing and take it to the next level. Tweak it just enough to be original, yet old fashioned enough that people believe in its success.

A free workshop opens up a wide expanse of advertising. Starting with television. Every cable company has a channel where you can list upcoming free events. You want to start doing this about four weeks out. It is amazing how many people actually watch that channel for stuff to do when they are bored. If you watch it once you are addicted; after that you just sit there watching the information flow across the screen waiting for the perfect event for you to attend. Sort of like watching a soap opera reenacting a train wreck.

Free workshops combined with book signings will get you interviews on the local morning and afternoon news/talk shows. Yes you may have to get out of bed at four in the morning to be there by five, but people are watching that early in the morning. Using your Smile and Dial attitude call and ask for the producer of a particular show and go through the same steps you went through for the book signing. After they book the interview submit to them a list of interview questions with the other requested documents. They won't stick to the script you provide them, but it does give them some guidelines.

These same free workshops with book signings will get you interviews on the local radio talk and college shows. Some of them will be call in and some will be studio. Studio is always better. Again approach them as you do everything else with a Smile and Dial attitude and let it rip. Have ready at their request the following from your publicity package: Your short bio for announcers, your ARC and your excerpt for the producers. Make arrangements to receive a video copy of any appearance and finally make arrangements for signed copies of the title to be distributed for office staff associated with the show.

If you have the lead time, at least four months, then you can use the local lifestyle scene to help promote your book. Find out who the book lifestyle editor is in the local happenings. Remember not to limit yourself to just the major publication, there are smaller publications in communities surrounding the main city. Contact them via the request form on their web sites. Make sure in your query that you list the appearances and free workshops you are giving in their area. The results of which are far reaching. They usually at least list you in their calendar of events, but I have seen it lead to a review of a book and an interview piece. That kind of exposure you can only get with a time investment and a great Smile and Dial attitude.

With all the work you are doing don't forget to submit queries to have excerpts of your book or short story posted as many places as possible. Again your Smile and Dial attitude will lead toward greater exposure. Query with your introduction. Your second sentence is about where you will be appearing and five words about what each event is for, then a simply worded request that they look

150

> Wear a gaudy necklace that hangs like a choker or a flashy, loud necktie during an interview. It attracts the eye and the viewer will look at your face.

at an excerpt for consideration. Your closing line is a thank you for their time and an invitation to contact you for more information about your upcoming events.

The last thing you can do is submit review packages to the local book sections of the periodicals in the area. This is generally a different editor from the contact for submitting information about your upcoming events. Book reviews are generally only done once a week for daily's and one a month for periodicals that publish less than daily. Make sure to review all of the submission guidelines for book review requests. The difference for this is in your query you mention your upcoming events, focusing on your free events to their public.

The electronic age is a wonderful tool for setting everything up and getting exposure quickly. It is the wonderful tool that provides instant gratification to a majority of its users. In the case of appearances, book signings or any other kind, a short sweet, emotionless e-mail cannot convey the same level of thanks and gratitude as a hand written note, and a small thank you gift for your

Pay it forward. Give back.

hosts. It is old fashioned, is a small monetary investment and a huge time investment. Just do it. It is something that not many people do. A card and gift are constant reminders to that professional, that you were kind and generous; it opens the door to other events not just with that person, but with others in their network.

151

Chapter Twelve: Using The Press
(Time and Money)

There are several types of announcements that you can use to inform the public about what is going on in your writing career. Each announcement may say pretty much the same thing, but are ideally personalized with a word or two for a specific purpose. First decide if you are promoting your book, your professional persona or one of your several other interests. Then personalize each one generally for the main subject, and then further for the actual character of the publication you want your press item to appear in.

Trade Announcement

A trade announcement is a short snippet that can be confused with a journalistic effort. This announcement is simply to let the world know something particular: You have a publisher, your web site is launched, you have won an award. The only subject in these announcements are that they say something about you or your book. This is tooting your own horn. You earned it so do it.

A trade announcement is written and presented in the same format as a newspaper article. It is short and sweet, less than a hundred words. It give the details as to the who, what, where, when, and why. So the broken record starts once again, search and research. There are places to post your trade announcement dependent on what the announcement is. You have your general places for books, but if you received an award for your volunteer work then you would publish it with your book stuffs, and then expand it to the other sites that specialize in volunteer work, making sure you sign off with your pen name and author of.... Prepare your trade announcements to meet all differing submission guidelines.

Toot your own horn! No one else will.

There are several periodicals that do trade releases. Of course the first place you are going to start is within your industry, but don't forget the local newspapers, coupon publications and everything else that has a print or web presence. Each department has a different editor for these things so make sure you send it to the right person. Confirm the delivery and follow the publication for the printing of it. Remember that trade announcements are not time sensitive, so most of the time they are published as space is available. You may have to follow for a while until yours pops. After it is printed, do what we call a clipping: Make a hard copy, scan it, including it in your promotional package, on your web site, and on your brag wall.

Sample Trade Announcement:

Be the Best!
(Catchy 3 word heading)

Want to be like Nora Roberts or Clive Cussler? *(Tag line less than 10 words)* They have been successful authors for years due to two simple things, a dream and a plan. Every author wants to be on the New York Best Sellers List, so why not your book? *(Mission statement with introduction)* Come join us on Friday, September 16, 2008 from 3pm - 5pm at the Birmingham Public Library 2100 Park Place, Birmingham, AL 35203. *(When and Where)* H. Christine Lindblom, will be sharing her insight on the book world and help you start a plan to turn your dream into reality. She will show you how to make your book appealing to not only the reader, but to the book stores that your future readers will be buying your book from. *(Name, and general purpose - 25 words or less)* This process will result in sales of your book and money in your pocket. *(What they will get from it)*

Now for your own trade announcement:

Tag line less than 10 words.

_____

_____

_____

Mission statement with introduction.

_____

_____

When and Where.

_____

_____

Name, and general purpose - 25 words or less.

_____

_____

What they will get from it.

_____

_____

Trade Shows

Trade shows are another great way to get the word out. Every trade show has at least one publication for the show. If it is a multi-day show, there are usually new publications each day. The Book Expo America (BEA) is the largest trade show in the United States for books. Book buyers, librarians, agents, producers, you name it, for our industry and they are there. *Publishers Weekly* puts out a printed trade publication every morning of the BEA and passes it out to everyone there. You pay for the space in the publication, but it is so worth it. Think of all the people you are going to reach with just a single announcement, on just one day of an event of that magnitude.

It never ends until you are ready to end it.

Now just as the book business has a trade show, so do all the other industries in the area. Some are bigger than others, but all of them have some sort of publication that allows you to place an announcement in them. Dog shows have their catalog, BEA has its daily flyer, gardening shows, quilting shows, cat shows, plastic conventions, sales conventions, educational conventions - the list is almost endless. Even if you have a vague connection in your book or work to an industry, massage that connection into something substantial that you can market.

Pull up a list of trade shows coming to your area and figure out where you can squeeze in. Go to their web site and look at what is available for you as an attendee and just as an advertiser. Look at what their theme is for the show and make your copy fall in line and support their theme. Look at their submission guidelines, and if you can talk to the person in charge of the project for details that aren't in their general postings. After you submit, confirm the arrival of your package and do the necessary follow up. Collect the clipping for your web site and promotional package. Remember that a majority of the time this is ad space you are paying for. There is almost no time investment except to find and decide where your money investment will net the best results. They do all the work for you.

Press Releases

Press Releases are used to announce an appearance or event that you are holding. There is a very specific format. It includes the Who, What, Where, When, Why and How. These are sent to anyplace that runs a calendar or events section of your periodicals. These need to be submitted at least six weeks before your appearance. There are several tutorials on line on writing press releases, and they support and contradict each other, so the rule to follow - use the style or combination of styles that best suits you and your writing styles. I tend to follow outline form where everything is clearly stated. I actually start my paragraphs with Where: and then the location. When submitting it that way I feel it is the easiest for copy and paste into printed copy. These are calendar announcements that have the information organized in such a way someone can easily cut and paste it into a calendar, yet enough information that they can write a short trade type announcement to fill space.

155

You have several places to submit press releases, unlike trade announcements which are subject specific. Press releases can go anywhere and should go as many places as you can get them. Start sending press releases six weeks before the event, but re-release them every week to the same agencies, up until the day of the event. As the event gets closer, say two weeks out, start resubmitting them two to three times a week. Make sure you send them to the correct department for press releases, as mentioned it is a calendar event, so send it to the correct editor.

Most of the news sites and community sites have calendars where you can enter the specific information directly. This is a time sink, but one that is well worth it. Those calendars are there for the public, they are promoted on your local news stations and radio stations. It is sort of a clearinghouse, but it is a targeted clearing house of events for people who are familiar with that area and trust the people promoting it. The more calendars that you put it on the higher the return on the search engine. Putting a calendar on your own site, helps people find you and where you are going to be. This is also a form of a press release.

You will have several press releases to choose from based on the submission guidelines for the individual publications. Make sure you keep a record of where you submitted them and who you submitted them to. Confirm the delivery of all the submissions and track their printing. Clip any printings for your promotional package and web site.

Your Press Release

(Short mission statement or title of event.)

CONTACT: This is who is hosting you and their contact information, e-mail and phone number.

WHAT: This is the type of event it is: Book signing, Panel discussion, Writing Workshop etc. and a short summary of what is going on. If you are having a panel discussion include the names and a short summary of their presentation. Start with the title of their portion of the discussion and 10 words or less for each portion of it. If it is a workshop make sure it has a title, and 10 words describing what people should get out of it.

WHO: This is a listing of who is presenting. It includes their name, title and the company they represent. It also includes a 10 to 15 word bio of each presenter.

WHEN: This is the date, the hours to and from.

WHERE: This is the location with a phone number

WHY: This is the mission statement of the entire presentation. No you can not write 'to sell books.' Your mission is to educate and entertain, so put that in so many words for the public.

FOR MORE INFORMATION: This is for more information directly from the participants. You should be the main contact information for this and allow the opportunity to make new contacts and find out directly what this group and region are interested in. Make sure to include your name, e-mail and business phone.

When planning to send out your press releases and trade release, don't forget to send out requests to have your work reviewed or endorsed by those places also. If you pay for advertising space they are more likely to review your work. Send your standard request for a review package to the periodicals and endorsement packages to the trade shows. Make sure to do all your follow up.

Chapter Thirteen: Evaluate Your Efforts
(Time)

Okay listen carefully. Knowing what works is just as important as what you do. Taking time to look at what your efforts are producing is the first step to time budgeting. Knowing the amount of time it takes to produce results of each item you try, is also important so you set yourself up for success. Instead of thinking you failed because there hasn't been enough time for the information to matriculate through the vast knowledge banks now available to us.

Remember that in 2010 it was recorded that 125 titles were released daily through the ISBN process, and that doesn't include those that were released privately or without an ISBN. This also does not include inner office publications, or textbook addendum. Without the registration process with the ISBN organization then there is really no way to track exactly how many titles are out there. Now let us add to that the ebooks and the plethora of methods and distribution for those that do not necessarily require an ISBN or a tracking system at all. So how are people going to know about you and your writings and how long is reasonable before they do?

Your blogs take between six and nine months of consistent, useful and searchable information before they become established. You can garner some faster results using a micro blog system such as Twitter to get it out a bit faster, but it still requires a lot of time and then if you don't keep it up or miss a single

> **If you want it, really want it, then you will make it happen.**

posting when you have people who are following it, you can lose a good percentage of your following. Well established blogs have been around for two or three years, have won awards, have valuable, popular and micro focused information or a good story line that is shared and passed around. Blogs gain sponsorship and notoriety from their content and their attitude. So once started it never ends until you are ready for it to end. Your blog host has different tools to help you track your audience that views your blog, right down to a twenty five mile area. Use them to find out how to target those regions most interested in you and your book.

Your web page is more stagnant, but it should be updated at least once a week. You have upcoming appearances, new short stories, new contests, new everything and your adoring fans want to know it all. Keep it exciting and keep it current. Remember that the adoring fans look at your reviews first, then your web page and then your blog. Your web hosting service has the same tools as does the search engines most people use. Learn how to use them to your advantage.

It is easy to track appearances, just ask where they heard about you and your book when they are in line.

To keep your workshops up to date and interesting pass out three by five cards at the beginning of your workshop. Then have them write a question on it that you didn't answer in the presentation. Answer them at end of the session – if there is one you don't know the answer to, go home and find the answer and then follow it up with an e-mail not only to that person but to the whole group. These are questions you incorporate into subsequent presentations, keeping you current and up to date.

Your interviews are easy to track; where you have an interview is what region is interested in you. Find out the demographics of the show, the broadcast area and ask for a copy of the interview and permissions to re post it to your web site. Then use the web site tracker to track who watches.

It is difficult to track snail mailings, emailings, and other form of bulk media communication, so you can simply have a form on your web site and in your dealings asking how they heard about you.

Constantly and consistently looking at your marketing and how it is affecting those around you is just good business. For the author in us that wants accolades, watching the tracking move from two cities, to five, to ten, to three hundred and fifty, and then by leaps AND bounds, gives you the same rush as a standing ovation at the *National Book Awards*.

Conclusion:

Whew! That was exhausting. I know. I have done this work and still continue to do it for several of my interests. The time is no longer where the local small town author, sits in the back of the local coffee shop, sipping coffee and is gawked at by the touristy passersby. There is so much to do and so little time. To tell the truth, writing is the easiest thing you will do in this new career of yours. It will still be your escape, your solace and your world that you share only with a chosen few until it is perfect. What it won't be is the reason you make money doing it, the marketing is. It seems like a lot at this time, but as mentioned before, pick two thing a quarter, and incorporate them into your daily tasks and before you know it, you will not even know you are doing it.

Now with the completion of ALL the exercises in this book and the start of getting everything set up and working, you have completed the two hardest, most tedious and most time consuming portions of this new career. ASSSS whole new world of challenges, hurdles and tasks will open up to you. The next biggest time sink you have is follow up. Making sure that everyone who was supposed to get something, received it, that it was correct and that they don't need anything else. This encompasses everything from the press package, and photos to the actual books or supplemental material that they need for the event or appearance. Then you have the deadlines, finish lines, and completions of your true passion, the subsequent books. Unless you are like me and wrote just one, this one hit wonder.

This system works. We have seen it work not only for authors, but coaches, editors, air conditioning companies, breeders, farms, yoga studios, art studios, photographers, wedding planners and so many others. In theory this method of publicity and marketing can work for any business, or trade, at any time. It is never stagnant, always morphing and always is easily kept up to date with the latest in technologies, information and help for the chosen industry. The plan is general enough to cover all the major bases and yet targeted enough to get a great return on the time and monetary investment you have made.

To end this book we will simply say:

Success is in the eye of the beholder.

As promised: When you complete this one, compare with your previous answers.

What is going on in your life right now? (List your top 5 priorities)

_____

_____

_____

_____

_____

Do you have a partner? (Spouse, girlfriend, boyfriend, fiance.)

    Yes   No

Do you have children?

    Yes   No

List 5 ways that marketing will affect them? (Think in both the positive and the negative. Such as, we will spend our summer vacations at book signings, but book signings only take a couple of hours, so look at all the neat stuff they are going to see along the way.)

_____

_____

_____

_____

_____

Are you going to keep your current job?

    Yes   No

Can you pay your bills and pay for your marketing if you work part time?

    Yes   No

Can you quit your job and become a full time author and marketing extraordinaire?

Yes   No

Describe what your marketing career looks like.

_____

_____

_____

_____

_____

_____

_____

_____

_____

_____   **163**

_____

List 5 things you expect to get our of your efforts.

_____

_____

_____

_____

_____

Was this just a fun project that you have completed and now you can move on?

Yes   No

Appendices

The Program

This book was written for two purposes:

Marketing is expensive and time consuming. The average writer doesn't have it in their budget to afford the few thousand dollars a quarter that a good publicist charges. This book guides you through all of the start up and gets you to a point where you can focus your publicist on that ten percent you don't want to do, when you hire one. All those chapters that say "Time" underneath are things that you can give to a publicist to do.

Marketing is expensive and time consuming. Yes, I have said that before. Most authors do not buy other authors' books, they are saving their pennies and hoarding their dimes to pay for the things they need starting from that cup of joe at two in the morning, to the web hosting package. They attend workshops to find out more information about how to be where you are. You are now their hero, their mentor, their goal. Where they will not necessarily buy your book, not because it isn't good, but maybe they just don't read that genre, they will buy books that help them further their career and guide them to get to where you are. *The Book Business Book* was created to help promoting authors offset some of their marketing costs. So how can this help you as an author?

Broken Glass publishing will sell you the book at 60% off the cover price, with a minimum order of ten books. This allows you to sell the book for as much as you want up to the cover price listed on the book. Where you may sell one or two of your fictional books at a workshop for writers, you can easily sell five or six of *The Book Business Book*, and you get to decide your own profit, your own discount and your own inventory.

If you are interested in ordering books please contact Virgie at virgie@ thebookbusinessbook.com.

Plagiarism

LEAD: One of the nation's most eminent psychiatrists has resigned his position at Harvard Medical School and as head of one of its major teaching hospitals after he admitted plagiarizing large sections of four papers he wrote in medical journals and textbooks, Harvard officials announced yesterday. [1]

plagiarize:
    to use and pass off someone else's ideas, inventions, writings, etc., as one's own. To take another's writings etc. and pass them off as one's own. (The New Lexicon Webster's Dictionary of the English Language)

Due to the advent and access to easily acquired and quoted information there has been a rise in plagiarism over the past years. In the article referenced above, it was the wealth of information whose origin was lost when it came to the final presentation of the work.[2] Plagiarism is as simple as the writer using an original written work but rearranging a few words or phrases. It is so much better the way someone else wrote it, so why change it to sound worse than what it is? This is a common question from students to writers. There are several different ways to rewrite the sentence or paragraph, but you still have to give credit. It is the idea, conclusion, or opinion that is protected as well as the facts. Most plagiarism is inadvertent and accidental. No matter, it can cost you your entire reputation, your writing career and a ton of money.

I am a fiction author and don't have to note history.

This statement is blatantly untrue. You don't have to note your sources in the traditional way of academic thought, but you do have to give credit. This is done in a variety of ways, the first in your acknowledgments, listing the people or organizations who helped you, the second is in a non-fiction historical summary at the end of the book and the third is disguised as a list of books for further reading.

Plagiarism bloodlettings occur with a dreary regularity. Every few months, a reporter or writer is caught copying a dozen paragraphs from a newspaper here or stealing a few choice lines from an obscure magazine there.[3]

In the advent of the 'instant gratification' and 'information overload' attitudes, it is easy to see why plagiarism is getting such attention. From the basics in our school rooms to the great authors such as Steven Ambrose, and university professors who miss the details, writers of all genres have to be extremely careful and meticulous to noting sources, in any creative and entertaining way possible. Fiction or non-fiction, plagiarism, even of ideas or popular thought, is rabid with the advent of the internet. Posting of articles, creative writing or short stories can be easily copied and pasted without effort. Finding such cases of plagiarism is time consuming, and little can be done, especially in the internet forum.

---

1   Altman, Lawrence, K., "Eminent Harvard Professor Quits Over Plagiarism, University Says", New York Times, nytimes.com, November 29, 1988

2   IBID
3   Plotz, David, "The Plagiarist. Why Stephen Ambrose is a Vampire.", Slate Magazine online. Posted Friday, Jan. 11, 2002, at 11:19 AM ET, http://www.slate.com/?id=2060618

So how do you avoid having your work plagiarized?

Be careful where you post. Check their security, ask questions about it and make sure that they are a reputable source and/or site. It can be a new publication but make sure it is secure. Print publishing is the most secure way to publish, as it is harder to copy and paste. Also, look for places to post your work that are part of a double opt-in epublication. It won't guarantee someone will take it but at least it is another layer of protection.

Writing is hard work. It is the responsibility of the writers to protect each other and respect each others' work by not plagiarizing. Just as if you purchased a book without a cover, authors do not get paid for that sale, plagiarism is the theft of something greater, a mind.

CPSIA information can be obtained at www.ICGtesting.com
Printed in the USA
LVOW100544151011

250605LV00001B/1/P

9 781934 603109